ALTERNATIVE VEGAN
International Vegan Fare Straight from the Produce Aisle

Alternative Vegan: International Vegan Fare Straight from the Produce Aisle
by Dino Sarma Weierman
ISBN: 978-1-60486-508-0
LCCN: 2009901382
This edition copyright ©2012 PM Press

PM Press
PO Box 23912
Oakland, CA 94623
www.pmpress.org

Layout by Daniel Meltzer
Cover art by John Yates

Printed on recycled paper by the Employee Owners of Thomson-Shore in Dexter, Michigan.
www.thomsonshore.com

Table of Contents

An Introduction

Chapter 1:

Chapter 2:

Chapter 3:

Chapter 4:

Chapter 5:

Chapter 6:

Index

An Introduction
Into My World

Whenever I get hold of a new cooking thing of any sort, I, like a gamer with the latest console and stack of new games, feel the need to use it as soon as it has been brought home. The day I bought myself a mortar and pestle, I came home that night, bashed up some coriander seeds, poured the little shards of flavor into a bowl, and then ground up some ginger and garlic with a few lumps of rock salt. Then, I heated up my much-loved old wok, which my mother had since she got married over thirty-five years ago and has seen the sharp side of a stirring spoon more times than I can count. When it was screaming hot, I poured in some oil, threw in some spices, and watched them pop and dance in their hot bath. I flung in the coriander seeds (now beautiful and ready to give the oil their all) and some sesame seeds and waited to hear the calls of the sesame seeds, exploding all over the inside of the wok and onto my freshly clean stove. I stirred in a can of beans and let it get to a full boil. Then I stirred in some cooked rice and indulged myself in my newly crafted dish, which I could not have made quite this way without my brand-new marble mortar and pestle.

She will see the seductive wafts of perfume that the spices wear. She will make even the most haughty garlic a smooth, creamy, salty paste. She will demand that the ginger cut her long, stringy hair so that my soup doesn't have little strings of ginger. Like a best friend, she will improve with the amount of time that we spend together, teaching me, giving selflessly of herself whenever I ask. She will joyfully sing to me as I respectfully run the spices through her relentless stones. And when the two of us are finished playing in our exuberant dance of joy, she

1

will then go back to her beloved corner of my utensil shelf, to lie in repose for the next time we speak.

This is what I want cooking to become for you. I want you to look at the recipes presented here and be as excited as a kid with a new toy. I want your heart to race, your mouth to water, and your pots and pans to sing to you as they bring together the elements of a good dining experience. I want you ready to plunge into a recipe headfirst, mouth wide open and ready to go. I want you to approach your food with the exuberance we reserve for eating outside. Their food will never be as good as yours, because only you know your palate.

When you get my book home—into your kitchen or onto your nightstand at home so you can pore over its pages before sleep and have beautiful, savory dreams while you sleep—I want you to imagine ways of changing what I have to suit your palate. Decide what you would like to tweak, and how it would be good-tasting to you.

Once you've got a good idea of where you'd like it all to go, get out there and do it! There's no need to worry, because all of these recipes have been tested many times over by different people of different skill levels. This is our labor of love to you, so that you may explore the gifts of nature's bounty. Now get that knife sharpened, your oven preheated, and that cutting board washed. It's time to cook.

V

For more information about my life, cooking and to listen to my podcast, please visit my personal blog at:

altveg.blogspot.com

To get in touch you can reach me at:

alternativevegan@gmail.com

A Note on Being Vegan

When Bob Torres first approached me about writing a book, I was a newly minted vegan and wasn't too sure of myself when it came to explaining my ethics. I just wanted to make delicious food and be left alone. I feel like I've learned a lot from him, and from the enormous community of vegans out there. I would cheerfully call these people my friends, and I'm privileged to have stood alongside them for as long as I have. Since I first wrote this book, I have understood more strongly what it means to be a vegan.

Veganism is a moral stance. It's a political statement. At its core, it states unabashedly that the exploitation of animals is wrong. It demands to know, "What is it about being human that elevates our needs above the need of animals?" Veganism is not a diet. It is not an environmental movement, although many vegans do care deeply for the environment. It is not about "personal choice," as I've heard so many times. It's understanding that your "choice" to use animals means that you deny the animals' choice in their own lives.

It's not whether the animals are given "cage-free" scenarios or allowed to roam about before their bodies are used. It's about taking a stand and saying that the use of animals is unethical. It's also not about single-issue campaigns, such as those of people who boycott furriers but wear leather shoes. It's about being ethically consistent and living a life based on your ethics.

Funny how when you make a reasoned, ethical stance, people question your sanity, but when you follow a religion, based on blind faith, they consider you admirable. I'd sooner follow my morals, that I've taken time to reason out than follow someone else's morals about a deity that may or may not have anything to do with my life. I would ask you to think it over, if nothing else.

"But don't plants have feelings?"

3

Try an experiment. Take a stick, and poke a tree. See what the tree does. Is it yelling and screaming? No. Try that on yourself now. Poke yourself (not someone else). Watch how that part of you reacts to it. You move away. You may (depending on how hard you poked yourself with a stick) even yell or make a noise of discomfort. That's how you can tell, empirically, that you feel pain, and the tree doesn't.

Furthermore, if you are so concerned about the plants' welfare, let's perform a little thought experiment. For that animal product that you're eating, there's something to the tune of 16 pounds of plants that need to go into the animal to produce 1 pound of flesh. Who's eating more plants now?

As a vegan, I frequently get statements such as, "But it would be too hard!" or "I hate tofu!" as if that is a valid excuse to continue the mass murder and mutilation of animals. It's not difficult. The sheer volume of food that exists in the plant kingdom would make you dizzy. Even if you have allergies, even if you hate tofu, even if you can't consume gluten, there are so many things out there for you to eat, that to list them off would take me volumes more books to even nick the surface. Eat all of that and then get back to me about hating tofu, or it being difficult.

From the time I was young, I never understood why people didn't know what I can eat, considering that their meals seemed pretty boring in comparison. Boiled vegetables, swimming in puddles of nondescript liquid. Some dead thing, slathered in some other dead thing, and topped with secretions. It was always the same meat, the same cheese, the same boiled veg. No wonder they couldn't figure out what I eat! Their diet is so boring that to fathom a giant chunk of said diet missing would be to limit yourself to the dregs of the lunch tray.

I prefer not to partake in that sort of lifestyle. From day to day, the foods I eat are varied, beautiful, and delicious because I know how to cook them properly. Becoming vegan meant that I could start exploring the variety of plants that are out there and use the techniques that I knew all along to make the food happen. It didn't involve long and painful sacrifice. That's not what going vegan is all about. Going vegan is about discovering the bounty that the plant kingdom has to offer and living that decadence without harming another sentient being.

Let me take you on an adventure to show you how to eat without relying on fake meats, tofu, tempeh, seitan, soymilk, or other such ingredients. Although I have no moral objection to people eating these things (in spite of my tongue-in-cheek rants about them), I do feel like new vegans tend to lean heavily on these packaged foods, bypassing the produce aisle. While you are still being morally consistent if you're having tofu scramble and tempeh bacon with a glass of soymilk, you're not looking past the starting point. I can show you how to eat a wider variety of foods and start relying on your instincts when it comes to your cooking.

And nobody had to get hurt.

A Note about Collaboration

This book is a labor of love from a large community of vegans. I may be the one with the author's credit, but this does not mean that I would take full credit for anything in here. Bob recognized my ability to cook early on, and encouraged me to compile a cookbook. My friends that live near me, for whom I have cooked on countless occasions, kept me motivated to continue to experiment with food. My friend Liza is fond of saying "Trust the chef!" whenever people give me odd looks while making something.

Our family friends John and Susan Casbarro let me raid their kitchens, their pantries, and their grocery shopping to churn out new and interesting things. Dana and Joel Ballantyne (and their daughter, who we all know as Noodle), two other vegans who live near me, along with Susan and John, would get together for impromptu "cook-ins." Random vegetation would appear, rice would be cooking, beans would be boiled, and we'd attack the kitchen at full tilt either at Dana's or John's place. I cannot count the messes we made together. They never let me help clean up, and they were always enthusiastic about their leftovers. All the while, regardless of the level of disaster, they kept coming back for more and more.

My mother let me shamelessly tap her considerable knowledge in cooking. I'd be underfoot all the time when she was in the kitchen. She would brag to all her friends that her son is such a talent in the kitchen, and they'd jealously glare at their own sons for not paying attention when mother cooks. I am quite sure that, by now, all of my mother's friends in the far-flung reaches of the globe know about her talented little kid (who's not so little anymore).

My second eldest brother would encourage me in the kitchen and have me cook for his friends when they came over. After tasting the food, he would shamelessly brag about his baby brother's cooking prowess.

We'd make unlikely dishes, like fettuccine with tomato sauce and diced potatoes, ramen noodles with Indian pickles, and random rice concoctions that were always so good.

My father was a willing guinea pig (animal testing is not vegan) for countless dishes I made. He would eat them with a smile and didn't complain even when they were disasters. When my mother dashed off to India for a year, and it was just the two of us, I would make him his favorite eggplant dishes, which he ate with relish. Little did he know that my brain was quietly taking notes on all of it and storing it away.

My sister and brothers were equally patient and forgiving with my culinary adventures. I've made some rank disasters in the past, which they would basically respice and eat. Even when I would make a simple dish, like pasta with garlic and olive oil and a diced tomato (quite delicious, if I do say so myself!), they'd crave exactly that thing and be willing participants in eating it.

My grandfather would spoil me senseless with delectable delights. Murukku (a South Indian snack), pakora, bajji, anything my little junk-food-loving tongue could ask for was mine for the feasting. My grandmother would swear up and down that he was going to ruin my health and doom me to being that way for life, but he would chuckle and give me more.

Then there are the people on the Vegan Freak forums. Bob invited me to get a cookbook done, and I started producing recipes quite rapidly. Unfortunately, being a college student living alone at that time made it difficult to ideally test about 90 percent of the recipes I was cranking out. Bob put the pressure on to get them tested. Instead of being a good Dino and actually doing the work myself, I ran to the forums and asked for help. Within an hour of posting the request for help, we had most of our first round of testers, eager to jump on board. With round two, it barely took one night to get many of the vegans from the forums to rush in and offer their help.

They tested the recipes as close to the original as possible, then popped onto the forum to give me excellent, detailed feedback. There were mishaps, such as when I messed up the wording of the instructions or forgot ingredients I had in the list on the instructions, and there was that garlic incident that I'd rather not get into. The omusubi was originally a disaster and a half. It was bland and lifeless. The pakoras were equally disastrous in the beginning. I won't even get into the pain that was the dipping sauce for the appetizers.

Yet, even with all of that, my vegan friends kept coming back for more. "More recipes!" they cried. They kept me motivated when I was feeling down about things in real life. They kept me wanting to keep showing them different and interesting things. They continued to rally around me to create. They inspired me with their trust. Here are people whom I've never met. They'll probably never get a chance to meet me, either. Based purely on the faith they have in my ability, they put their dinners on the line.

There was the IRC chat room, too. The vegans hanging out there would ask, "Dino—I have a can of black beans, some leftover vegetables from that party I was at where they only served a stupid not-vegan dip with raw vegetables, and some rice. What do I do?" I would respond with, "Got any peanuts, walnuts, pecans, onions, or garlic?" I'd get a "Sure, I've got it all." I would crank out a recipe right there on the spot. Often it was a combination the person hadn't considered.

Then, the person would dash off to the kitchen, cook whatever it is I said to cook, and come back and rave about it to the others, who all would demand that the person share. I would log on, see some part of someone's username in the chat room, and decide to create that person a dish based on that name. The person would be honored and make the dish.

I am not an island—I am the product of the thousands of years that vegetarians the world over have been cooking. I am a culmination of all the friends, family, animals, and people I've met all my life. I have the ability to create because there is beauty in this world and I can appreciate it.

What does all of this mean?

It means that I, as the "author" of the book am no more solely responsible for the creation of it than you who read it. If it weren't for the fact that you need something like this, I would have had no reason to produce it. If Bob hadn't spotted my abilities at the time he did, I wouldn't have bothered to compile this mad stack of ravings. If it weren't for the fact that the world is such an amazing place, with so much beauty and so many adventures waiting to happen, I would not be the person that I am. I don't own these ideas—they're all of ours to share. So take this book and share it!

In that spirit of sharing, I would like it if you would take this book, and take copious notes as to your experiences. There are margins on the pages for a reason! Go ahead and mark it up, so that it works for you. There are times when a particular recipe works in my kitchen, or in the kitchen of a tester, but not in yours. Make a note about how you made it work for you, and tell me about it! That's the beauty of projects like this one: they are shaped by the experiences of real people, who share their expertise.

Basic Kitchen Tools Guide

This is the "what you need" section. Also known as "Dino is a diva meanie-head who wants us all to be like him and he hates us all and let's go scream at him."

I was being facetious with the subtitle, but it's a sort of mentality that I used to have when a cookbook told me that I need a tool or something along those lines that I didn't have. Here I give you the heads-up as to the bare essentials, how not to spend a fortune on it, and how to take care of it so that you're not cursing me out on the phone next week when your cast iron skillet turns into a rusted hole-riddled thing. So let's get started.

On Skillets

First and foremost thing to discuss is the cast iron skillet. It's perfect for frying. It's perfect for cooking. It'll get your vegetables roasty and toasty, and after using it for a while, it becomes (through what I know to be magic) nonstick. It's dark and heavy and slippery slick. It's also cheap. You can generally find one at the hardware store for less than $12, and if treated right this thing will last you forever. A good, seasoned nonstick skillet is worth many times its weight in (cruelty-free, sweatshop-free, evil-corporation-free) gold. Hold onto it for dear life (when it's not blazing hot), as your family members will jealously eye it if they know how you got those stunning results on the dinner table.

To care for your new best friend (sorry, dogs, but you don't know how to get those herbed potatoes all crusty) is far simpler than you'd think. After you're done with your cooking, drain off any excess fat from the pan. Sprinkle some kosher salt into the pan. Let it sit for a minute or so, scrub it around with a paper towel, and discard the salt and the paper towel. Rub in some extra oil, and leave it alone. Don't wash it. Don't put it in the dishwasher. You want to develop that fat coating, and washing it will just wash away all your work.

Some people are lucky enough to inherit a cast iron skillet, and those people can go away because I'm jealous. Others, like me, need to start from scratch. Now what? Internet! Go online, and find a preseasoned cast iron skillet. They will tell you up front that it's been seasoned from vegetable sources, and you're set. Cooking.com has a 10.25-inch skillet seasoned by Lodge that's $17, and they say right there that it's from a vegetable oil blend that's heated in industrial ovens.

For the more DIY types, go to the local hardware store, snag a cast iron skillet for $10 to $12, and swing by your local grocery store. Why? You need shortening. I'm really not joking here. We don't have industrial strength ovens that can force vegetable oil in its unsaturated form to accept the fat properly. Besides, with the shortening, you can go home and make your own puff pastry later on.

Go home and preheat your oven to 275° F. Rub the shortening on the pan. Wear plastic food service gloves (or a sheet of parchment paper to help keep your fingers clean), because I don't think you'll be too fond of solidified fat sitting in the crevices of your hands. Make sure to coat every inch of the pan's insides (not outsides) with the grease.

You might even want to overdo it and have a little bit of excess. This can't harm the pan.

Once coated, put your pan into the oven and let it sit there like that for about 20 minutes. Take out the pan and pour off the extra grease. Put it back into the oven and reduce the heat to 200° F. Leave it there for 5 or 6 hours, or overnight. Do not waste the oven's heat while this is going on. Take a few 6-quart pots that are oven safe, and pour in one variety of bean into the bottom of each pot. Fill them with water, leaving about 5 inches of headroom, and put on a lid. Put them into the oven with the skillet so that you have hot cooked beans in the morning, along with a seasoned skillet. The low heat of the oven will allow the beans to cook slowly, as in a crock pot. Keeping the water just below boiling point will prevent too much water evaporating as steam.

On Knives

If it were a more perfect world, they would have figured out how to clone me, and you could have your very own Dino to cook for you all the time. But we're not in a perfect world. So, you have this book instead.

Similarly, in an ideal world, we would all be able to afford top-quality knives. We'd go to our local knife sharpener, who would sharpen our knives for us, and we'd have beautifully working knives all the time.

Enter: reality. You're a college student who couldn't give a flying cabbage about perfect situations. You want something you can afford five minutes ago, and you want it yesterday, darn it. You're a single mother without the time, energy, or patience to go trawling through second-hand stores, stalking the knife section. You have actual bills to pay. So what do you do? You get what you can afford immediately, move on, and tell me to cram it.

Don't do this. If you cannot afford top-quality knives, just go the next best step down—never-needs-sharpening knives. Before the real chefs reading this come chasing me with aforementioned knife for such blasphemy, hear me out. A dull knife is a dangerous thing. If it slips, it will cut you (but not the vegetables) badly. And your hands, being the most sensitive parts of your body, will not thank you for this mistreatment. Instead of asking you to blow $100 to $300 on a top-quality knife that you can't or won't care for, I'd prefer that you just get the never-needs-sharpening kind and move on. You can generally get one for a few dollars. Get a 12-inch chef's knife, and move on.

But I still wish you'd get a good one.

On Pots

This is where you cannot compromise. Don't worry about brand names, celebrities on the cover, the fancy garbage they try to tell you about the pot that means nothing to you, and so on. So much of it is marketing, rather than actually showing you differences in the meal you'll end up serving. If you're in a professional setting, you'll have to invest in the top-quality pots and pans, and do not have room for compromise.

This would also mean that you have perfectly calibrated stoves, top-quality steel counters that can handle the high heats these pots get to, and equipment fitting of those pots. You aren't in a professional kitchen, though; you're at home, and you need to be prepared to work within the constraints of your own budget.

I would rather have you find an OK pot that you will use and can afford rather than you tell me to go sod off and use a horrible one. So in that spirit of compromise, let me tell you this: conventional wisdom is anything but.

What do I mean? Ideally, you'd all have copper cooking pots. They're excellent conductors, and they hold heat well. Meanwhile, I don't have a full-time maid to clean them, which is what using copper cookware would require. They take stains extremely well, and hold on to their stains. Copper cookware is very expensive. Once I make my first billion, I'll be sure to get out there and buy copper cookware for all my friends and all you readers out there. Until then, I'll have to keep looking.

Then you've got cast iron. I love cast iron with all my heart, but frankly, I can't be bothered to wait for a cast iron Dutch oven to heat up. I want something that won't make me cringe at the gas bill every time I heft it out. Ideally, all my cookware would be cast iron, so that I can get that perfect distribution of heat, and the maintenance of heat that cast iron offers. Unfortunately, I'm not a power lifter. I also don't have an unlimited budget to spend on gas for the stove.

Then they have all the fancy metals that a stockpot can come in, and they use all these fancy terms like "sandwiched" and "anodized" and other such rot. I'm sure that someone out there somewhere has bought this sort of thing and noticed a significant difference in the quality of the food they turn out. When I meet that someone, I'll let you know. You as the home cook won't really notice that much of a difference. All that stuff is just...stuff to justify the exorbitant price. I'm not producing world-class cuisine for the Emperor of America's mom. I'm making myself a pot of soup because I'm hungry, and I want to eat something comforting to me. I'm not sitting in my million-dollar restaurant and hoping that some VIP is going to throw me some piddling praise. I'm making a pot of pasta with some simple olive oil and basic ingredients.

For me, the home cook, a good, heavy-bottomed, large 12-quart stockpot does wonders for me. I can boil water quickly. I can sauté my onions in the pot till they're a golden, caramel-y brown, then trust the heat to sustain the sweat later on. I can control the heat enough so that the soup sustains a nice, steady simmer. I can pour in some oil and fry up some delicious, crispy yucca fries. That's what I care about.

Get yourself a pot larger than you think you need. The extra space allows for steam to move around and prevents bubbling over when you have starchy ingredients. Get a pot that feels heavy on the bottom but not so heavy that you can't lift it easily. Carrying a steaming hot pot of doom will be your own downfall if it's too heavy. Get one with metal handles so that you can transfer it to the oven if needed. And make sure the pot has a nice tight-fitting lid. It shouldn't run you more than $20.

My mother has always been a huge fan of second-hand stores, garage sales, rummage sales, and other such reuse initiatives. If I tell her I got something on sale at the store, she'll go out on a Saturday morning, find pretty much the same thing, and show me up by getting it for a fraction of what I paid on the taxes for the thing I bought. She'll shoot me a smug look and say something like, "You won't outdo the master, my dear." I then hang my head and return the thing.

My grandfather was fond of saying, "Only a fool learns from his own mistakes. A wise man learns from the mistakes of others." Let's combine the wisdom of both my mother and her father (my grandfather). Get out to those second-hand stores, the thrift stores, the yard sales, the rummage sales, the swap meets, and all the rest. Get onto websites like freecycle.org, which are all about sharing what we don't need with others. Be on the lookout for a bargain, because you will most assuredly find one.

I don't think I own any cookware with a pedigree. They're all of indiscriminate origin, dug up by my mother in her adventures. Why not make it an adventure? Cooking is certainly an exciting adventure—why not get yourself into it headfirst? When you do find that real bargain, you'll have earned bragging rights with me and my family. Just don't brag to mom, because she'll promptly show you up and send you packing with a whole bunch of food.

There you have it. Those are the three essential parts to a kitchen. With those three basic tools, you can produce a dizzying array of impressive and delicious foods. I will go into more detail about other useful products in the next section.

Cooking Techniques

If sautéing makes you sweat...

Different cooking techniques will bring out different aspects of your food. Depending on the flavor and texture of the food that you desire, you will be using one or many of the techniques I have presented. I'll explain briefly the reasons for using each method with its preparation instructions. The reason I'm spending time on this is not just so I can shorthand the techniques later—it's more about giving you an arsenal of tools for your vegan toolbox.

By understanding the different techniques, you will first and foremost be a more skilled cook. More than that, you will also become a more independent cook. If you know what a particular technique is and see it being grossly messed up, you can catch on to that error quickly, and you will know better.

An example of this is when I was younger and was making a pot of soup for my sick sister. The recipe was beautifully shown in the picture next to it, and I wanted it to come out just right. Right there in the beginning, when it called for 5 tablespoons of salt to be sprinkled over my 3 cups of sweating vegetables, alarm bells went off in my head. I knew from watching the food channel that sweating happens at low heat, and with just a little bit of salt.

This leads me to a note about this cookbook. I keep repeating that you should do things that suit you so that you will want to keep cooking. If you see something in here that seems a bit extreme for your liking, trust your instincts and cut back on it. If you think that a pound of beans is going to be way too much for your family to finish, you're most likely right. (However, to be fair, I have seen a pound of beans disappear, like lightning, before my very eyes when I have cooked at friends' houses.)

I tend to err on the side of more salt, fat, and chile than a majority of people are comfortable with on this side of the pond. If something seems like it'll burn off the first layer of your tongue, cut back on the heat to suit your needs. I would think nothing of flinging a few tablespoons of red chile flakes into a pot of soup—that's just how my family eats. I also wouldn't mind having a heavily-spiced snack just before an equally heavily-spiced meal. Not everyone will be comfortable with that.

As long as you give yourself permission to experiment, you'll be fine.

Sautéing

Sautéing is specifically meant for drawing out the sugars from aromatics (such as onions or bell peppers) and other ingredients, and to get that food browned. It's a high-heat cooking method that yields a concentrated flavor that's slightly sweet. To sauté a vegetable of any kind, start preparing the vegetables. The French call the arrangement of your ingredients *mise en place*, and it's one of the first things that you will learn in a cooking school.

Have all your ingredients cut up into small pieces. Try to keep them as uniformly sized as possible, so that everything gets cooked evenly. If I were to make a hierarchical list about the importance of cutting, I would begin with uniformity in size. Too many times there will be different-sized chunks in the pot, all of which cook at different times, and the end result is ghastly. Do the best you can to get the pieces the same size. Have them arranged in front of you in an area near the stove. Also arrange any spices you'll be using, in the order that you add them to the oil, close at hand as well. Open any jars, bottles, or other containers, and have spoons ready to measure out your amounts of spices.

Turn your stove to the highest setting and put on a wide, shallow frying pan. Coat the bottom of the pan in about 3/4 inch of oil, and heat it until a little wisp of smoke escapes the surface. Immediately toss your vegetables to the hot oil. Once the vegetables are in the pot, stir them around to evenly coat all the pieces in the oil. You want the pieces looking shiny.

Once all the ingredients you want to sauté are evenly coated with oil, sprinkle in a little salt, and any of the dry spices you will be using—such as turmeric, curry powder, or any other dry spice—and stir all the ingredients in the pan to coat them evenly in the spices. Reduce your heat to medium-high. Forgetting to turn down your heat will result in burned spices.

Leave the ingredients sitting in the pot for 2 to 3 minutes or longer, depending on the recipe, until the desired brownness is achieved. You may deglaze the pan after this step for a rich sauce to form around the vegetables.

This basic sauté gives you an excellent starting point for any number of vegetables you want to cook. It works well for dark leafy greens, root vegetables, and beans. This would also be an outstanding point to start a soup. Oh no, I'm getting hungry. Let me go hammer out some baby spinach in this sauté, and I'll come back to show you how to deglaze. I promise I'll be back. In the meantime, what are you waiting for? Get out a pot, and sauté yourself some lovelies.

Deglazing

Deglazing is a method of loosening up the sugars in the bottom of a pot or pan. Usually, it is a step performed after sautéing, but this is not always the case. Deglazing helps liberate any flavors that are lurking about in your pot or on the surface of ingredients, dissolving them in the liquid. After you have sautéed your vegetables or aromatics in the pan, you may deglaze the pan with alcohol, juice, water, stock, or other wet ingredients. This is one of the essential techniques to have, as it will prevent your spices from burning. Wet heat is gentler than dry heat because water will not rise above its 212° F boiling point. Your metal pot, on the other hand, will get far above that. OK, I'll shut up and get on with it.

Other wet ingredients would be things like tomatoes, cooked beans with some of the cooking water, and even fresh fruit. Citrus is a wonderful bet for deglazing, since it leaks out its juices so quickly and coats the other ingredients so well. You may have even been deglazing your recipes all this time, but just didn't know what to call it! Now you've got a fancy technique to impress your friends. Use other wet ingredients when you would like to deglaze something that's only aromatics. If all you have in your pot is garlic and onion and some herbs, tomato would be your best bet. Deglaze with liquid when there are other vegetables in the pot already. These two rules aren't

hard-and-fast, but they do help form a basis for deglazing.

To deglaze with a liquid, sauté the vegetables as you normally would. Turn the heat back up to high. Wait 15 to 30 seconds for the pot to catch on that the heat has been increased. You should hear the vegetables begin to sizzle excitedly, telling you that they're ready for what you're bringing. Pour in about a cup of liquid into the pan and quickly begin to scrape down the bottom of the pan with a wooden spatula to free up all the little bits of browned goodness that got stuck to the pan. If it looks too dry to be able to scrape up all the bits, add in another 1/2 cup of liquid, and keep scraping. You'll have to work even more quickly if you're using alcohol, because alcohol evaporates more quickly than water. For an impressive trick, under safe conditions (no loose sleeves, no flammables nearby, fire extinguisher close by), after you've added the alcohol, you can remove it from the heat (and turn off the stove, please) and take it to the table. With the stick of a long lighter, set the surface of the alcohol on fire, and watch the ooohs and aaahs. The flambé technique does little to actually add any flavor and is more for show than anything of significance. Use it on special occasions.

A very short time after beginning to deglaze, you should start seeing the added liquid get thicker and thicker. When it's gotten thick enough to cling to the vegetables quite possessively but still coat the stirring spoon, you're done. The liquid should all be about as thick as a rich gravy.

When you want to deglaze with a wet ingredient, have that ingredient diced or minced ahead of time. Sauté the vegetables as normal. Turn the heat back up to high. When you hear your vegetables (in this case aromatics) sizzle and sing, quickly add your chopped up wet ingredient, and stir. Keep stirring for about a minute. Reduce the heat to medium, and let the mixture cook for 5 to 10 minutes, depending on the ingredient.

Sweating

Sweating is a gentle method of cooking vegetables that allows the flavors to slowly leak out of the vegetables and into the surrounding fat. It's a simple method because it doesn't involve too much "babysitting" like sautéing and deglazing. It's also ideal for beginning cooks because it doesn't hold as high a risk of burning something. If you're starting out as a cook, sweat your vegetables in lieu of sautéing them the first couple of times you try out a new or unfamiliar recipe. It will save a lot of fires and frustration!

The classic example of sweating vegetables is the basis of many soups: *mire poix*, which is usually carrots, onions, and celery. To begin, chop up all the pieces of vegetables into roughly 1/2-inch cubes. You want all the pieces to be as close to the same size as possible. When they're chopped, each vegetable should measure about a cup.

Once you have them all evenly chopped, prepare yourself a *bouquet garni* (bundle of herbs) using a small bunch fresh parsley, 2 or 3 sprigs of thyme, and 2 bay leaves (or whatever fresh herbs you like), and tie them up together with a piece of heat proof string. You may use a dried bay leaf, but the parsley and thyme should be fresh.

In a large stockpot, pour in some oil, until there is about 1 inch of oil in the bottom of the pot. Turn the heat up to medium-high and wait for the oil to heat. You may be nervous about placing your hand over the heating fat, so here's an easy trick to check the temperature of the oil. Take a chopstick or the thin end of your wooden spoon and poke the bottom of the inside of the pot, almost like you're using a long thermometer to take the oil's temperature. Let it sit there for 10 seconds or so. If you see little bubbles forming around your stick, the oil is just the right heat.

When the oil reaches optimal heat, pour in the combination of vegetables. Stir to combine, so that every piece of vegetable gets coated in the hot fat. Sprinkle in some salt and stir to combine once more. Reduce the heat to a lower setting, but not the lowest, and put the stockpot lid on. For a new cook, and even some experienced ones, this may be a nerve-wracking moment for you. But remember that the vegetables are at a relatively low heat.

Wait for a minute and listen to what you hear in the pot. Is it sizzling away? If so, the pot is too hot, and the temperature needs to be reduced. Reduce the temperature to a lower setting and open up the lid to vent off the excess heat. Stir the vegetables and spread them out flat. Put the lid back on and listen again. You should just barely hear noises coming out of the pot. It will sizzle, but only gently.

Once you've found the optimal temperature, leave the sweat to sit there in the low heat for 10 to 15 minutes. Every 5 minutes or so, come back in and stir the vegetables to redistribute the flavors. When you're done stirring, make sure to lay them flat in one layer again to promote even cooking.

After 15 minutes of cooking, the vegetables will be soft and ready to take in anything you can give it. Pour in about 1 quart (or liter) of stock and let it come up to a full boil. At this point, put in your bouquet garni, and the rest of the ingredients for your soup. You can use anything from vegetables (green leafy vegetables are always good), or even beans or other legumes.

Some popular sweats—like the *sofrito*, the *mire poix*, and the ginger-garlic-onion mixture of India (as yet unnamed, but it'll have its day in the spotlight!)—are so popular that they form the basis of a dizzying variety of dishes. Bear in mind that a sweat is not a sauté. It is a gentle form of cooking. Sautéing is delicious in a variety of foods, but it doesn't give the food enough time to leak out its flavors into the oil.

"Popping" Whole Spices

Throughout the book, you'll see me refer to getting oil very hot, adding whole spices, and waiting until they pop. What this means is that the whole spice cooking in the fat should explode, releasing its essential oils into the surrounding fat. It's a potent method of flavoring a savory dish, and I use it often. There are a few points to remember, and you will be popping away like mad in no time!

For one thing, don't expect this to be clean and neat. Even my deepest stockpots

manage to get a few stray seeds out of the pot and onto my counter, my hair, my face (ouch), or the surrounding stove. Those spices are going to go out with a bang, and they'll let you know, painfully, if you're not careful. For me, this is the most thrilling and exciting cooking method of all time. The end product is so delicious, and things move *fast*, so preparation is a key component. I am completely serious on this one. It's fun, but you want to be safe, and you don't want to waste money on burned spices.

I've watched little old grannies transform into superheroes with lightning-quick, and deft (if a bit wrinkled) hands. As a little boy, I perfected the technique of the "grenade method" of spicing. I watched my mother and aunts do it, and I do it myself. I myself have startled my mother's friends as they watched me transform, in the space of 5 minutes, a pot of humble, boiled lentils into a dark, smoky, soupy, kind of gravyish, sort-of-hot but oh-so-good pot of love.

Before you try this, make sure you have a clean kitchen, free of stray children, pets, or (in the cases of married folk) spouses. Have plenty of counter space ready. Make sure you've got on a full apron. Clear the room and warn your friends. You're in for the ride of your life. If you own a splatter screen (a piece of wire mesh with a metal ring around it that you can hold over things that tend to splatter), get it ready to go.

Before starting, have ready 1 teaspoon of cumin, 1 teaspoon of mustard seed, and a handful of curry leaves. Have a chopped onion sitting in a bowl in eager anticipation. Have your salt shaker next to the onion bowl, and have a teaspoon of turmeric at the ready. Next to the onions, place about 1 tablespoon minced ginger and 2 cloves of garlic, finely minced. Behind the onion bowl, have 2 medium tomatoes chopped evenly into small pieces at the ready. Behind the bowl of tomatoes, have a pound of cooked lentils, soaking in about 2 cups of their cooking liquid. The lentils will be soaking while they wait to be added to the pot.

Here's how it works. In a large wok, get about 3 tablespoons of oil screaming hot. You want a little wisp of smoke to escape the surface. Once it's hot like that, stand slightly back, with a small amount of the spice you would like (in this case the cumin and mustard seeds) in your hand. You wait for the smoke. You see it. Bingo. Fling the spices dead center into the wok and jump back. If you have the splatter screen, now would be the time to employ it.

The spices will begin to explode very shortly. Once you hear them popping like crazy, fling in the curry leaves, ripping them in half as you go. As soon as the curry leaves explode, immediately throw in the onion, ginger, and garlic. Sprinkle about 1 teaspoon of salt and 1/2 teaspoon of turmeric. Stir immediately to coat in the fat. Cook at very high heat until the onions are softened but not browned. This should be about 1 to 2 minutes.

Throw in the tomato and stir to coat in the fat. Let it cook at the high heat, making sure that you stir it frequently, for 1 to 2 minutes. When the tomatoes have broken down a

bit, pour in the pound of cooked lentils that you'd soaked in the cooking liquid along with their liquid. The water will boil almost instantly. Stir, and then scrape down the wok (remember deglazing?) to release the brown bits from the bottom of the wok. When the water comes to a full rolling boil, reduce the heat to a simmer, and let it sit that way until you're ready to serve it. You can eat it immediately, or later. I choose now, with rice.

Pasta Cooking Guide

Pasta can be a fun and interesting way to add some zing to your consumption of grains each day. There are a dizzying variety of shapes, colors, and sizes in the pasta world, and I will leave it to your local store to show you those, as I don't have the time to go into all of them. I will, however, give you a baseline for cooking pasta, from which you can build your own dishes using different shapes and ingredients, based on what you can find. Even the most basic garlic, oil, and salt pasta is a treat.

First and foremost, you should make sure that you are cooking your pasta (regardless of the amount) in plenty of water. If you're making 1 pound (1/2 kilo) at a time, use 6 quarts (or liters) of water. If you are making 1/2 pound (250 grams), you should still use 4 quarts (or liters) of water. If you are making more than a pound, cook the extra pasta in a separate pot with its own 4 to 6 quarts. Why? There are a variety of reasons. For one thing, the water is going to receive the starch from the pasta. When you have a high quantity of starch in a small amount of water, the water will thicken up, and start forming bubbles. Those bubbles will then start stacking up on each other, and before you know it, you've got boil-over, and a disgusting burned smell when the starch burns on the hot stove. For another thing, those starches are responsible for sticky pasta. If you've ever had mushy rice with nothing on it, you'll know about how sticky starch can get. Using a large quantity of water gives the pasta enough space to move around and prevents sticking. Finally, you do it because I said so.

Another thing to remember is to liberally salt the water (salty like the sea). Why? This is the only chance you'll ever have of getting the pasta to take some salt in. Salt loves water dearly, and will cling to water as much as it can. When this clingy pair meet pasta, the three form a sordid love triangle of flavor. It's a beautiful thing. What happens when you don't salt your water? The starches on the surface of the pasta aren't as receptive, and don't let the salt in. Also, in the absence of water, the salt is like a rejected lover; it just lies there and doesn't do much of anything. Salt becomes the party pooper. Salt your water.

If you're cooking pasta and you're nervous about sticking, citrus can be your friend. Oil, in its slippery slickness, cheats you out of proper pasta, because having oil on the surface of the pasta doesn't let it take to sauce well. The sauce, much like the rejected salt, will sit there in a pool by itself, shunned by the smoother, slicker oil. Instead, when you add lemon (about 1 tablespoon per 4 quarts) your pasta tumbles around in joy in the pot, and marries rather well with the sauce when you're done.

Draining pasta can be a tricky thing. You don't want it to be so well drained that it's dry, because then it'll stick together. You also don't want it too wet, because that will dilute the flavors in your sauce. Instead, you have to find a happy medium that lets the pasta be mellow, but not so mellow that it falls down. When you pour your pasta through a colander to strain it, just shake the colander once or twice, and pour it into a receptacle immediately. You'll have just enough water hanging around to keep the pasta chaste, and enough will evaporate off that the sauce can come in and do its work.

You can make sauces as you're waiting for the water to boil. This is actually the perfect time to do so, as your pasta, the main attraction, is a big diva. It will not be kept waiting. Sauce waits for pasta, but not the other way around. By the time you drain your pasta, you should be immediately ready for the sauce to meet the pasta on the serving dish. The moment that the pasta slides out of the colander and onto a serving dish is when it's most receptive to flavor. After a long bubble bath in the boiling water, it'll take anything that comes along. Make this anything be the flavor, and you won't be sorry!

Now comes the part about cooking time. If I give people a time, they're going to set a timer to that exact time, end up over- or undercooking their pasta, and then call me the next day to curse me out. Barring that, I will get some choice phrases via e-mail, beginning with things I'd rather not repeat in print. This is a cookbook, not my middle school playground.

The only way to tell if your pasta is done is to taste it. There are some pastas that take 2 or 3 minutes to cook, and others that take much longer. You have to test it. Pull out a noodle with a slotted spoon and bite into it. Throwing it onto random kitchen spots will just give you a messy kitchen, and you still won't know if it's cooked. You have to touch it and taste it. Give the noodle a little squeeze. Does it give at all? Does it feel hard in the center? Bite into it, and chew it around. Does it taste cooked? Can you see completely uncooked pasta in the center? Do you think it could do with more time? Are you going to be cooking it some more in some other dish? In the recipe below, I'm going to give you a rough cooking time. Do not use this as a hard-and-fast rule and leave me nasty phone calls. I'll just send them all to Bob, and he can handle it. Know your food.

I've prattled on forever, so let me get to the program. Boil the water in a large stockpot over the highest heat that your stove has. You will not be turning down the heat again. You want it to be at a full, rolling boil. Sprinkle in salt by taking your salt shaker and generously sprinkling in salt from one side of the pot to the other until you've sprinkled "all over" the pot's surface. This is the method I find simplest, which is why the salt isn't a measurement. The salt will dissolve almost instantly.

When the salt does dissolve, dip a clean spoon into the water, and take out some of the water. Blow on the surface of the water to cool it down, and taste it. If it tastes salty enough to you (it should be as salty as sea water), you've salted it perfectly. If it's too salty, pour out some of the water, and replace it with fresh water.

Once the water is at the proper salt and boil, put a wooden spoon in the pot. Pour in your pasta in one quick motion, and immediately start stirring so that it doesn't make a giant clump in the bottom of your pot. Stir until the water comes to a full boil. Pour in your lemon juice.

Your pasta will begin looking larger and be more flexible as time goes on. Again, this is not a hard-and-fast rule, but wait about 5 minutes after the water has come to a full boil, and begin testing your pasta by removing a noodle or two from the pot with a slotted spoon. Blow on the surface of the noodle to cool it down. When it's cooled down, bite into the noodle, and see if it seems done enough. Squeeze it between your thumb and forefinger to see if it gives enough. It probably won't be done yet, but you will now have a starting point from where you can see where the pasta is going. Ladle out some of the pasta water into a serving dish and swish it around. This warms up the plate. Dump out the water. Ladle on a second washing of this water to maintain that heat. Leave it there. Put a colander in the sink.

Test your pasta again. If it's not cooked to your liking (note: your liking, not mine or anyone else's), let it go for another minute and test again. Keep going like this, tasting and waiting for a minute or so until your pasta is done to your liking. Dump out the pasta and the water into the colander, and shake once.

As soon as your pasta is shaken out, feel free to throw it in a bowl, and add your herbs, spices, sauces, oils, or anything else you like to eat on pasta. An important thing to remember is that you want to add the sauce while the pasta is still hot, to facilitate maximum absorption of the flavors. You may be tempted to toss on some oil before you add your sauce. Resist this temptation. All it's going to do is give the pasta a slippery surface to which sauce will not adhere. Just have your sauce ready when your pasta is done. You have plenty of time to prepare, especially since the water takes so long to come up to a boil.

Rice Cooking Guide

If you're going to be making rice regularly, I really wish that you would go out and get yourself a rice cooker. You can often find one in a thrift store. If you can't find one used, a new one shouldn't run you more than $30 for a basic model.

Not convinced, eh? I tried. What I'm about to tell you breaks most major rules for cooking rice the traditional way, which is to start it off with a quantity of water, and allow that water to absorb into the rice. Unfortunately, that traditional method often leaves me with a burned pot, ruined rice, and hours of cleaning. It also manages to demolish my manicure every single time. Let's avoid the drama, shall we?

Start off with 1 cup uncooked long-grain brown or white rice. I personally prefer brown rice, because when you cook it, the grains are far more forgiving than white rice. Because they take longer to cook, you've got a fair bit of wiggle room when you're in the process of boiling it. Brown rice is also better for you. It retains the high fiber and nutrients that rice is good for.

In a medium-sized pot, pour in the cup of rice and about 5 cups of cold water. Sprinkle in 1 teaspoon of salt. Put the pot on your stove, and turn it up to high heat. Let the water come to a full rolling boil. Reduce the heat to medium-high. Let the water continue to boil. In about 30 to 45 minutes, the rice should be cooked. Test a grain and see if it's cooked to your liking. If it is cooked, the rice is finished boiling.

In a colander, drain the rice of the excess water. If you're going to put it in the fridge to use later, toss it with a little bit of oil and put it away. Otherwise, feel free to use it immediately. Either way, your rice is finally done!

If you're using white rice, the rice should take roughly 20 minutes to cook through. Test the rice at halfway in to the cooking, to make sure that you don't end up with mushy rice. If you do end up with mushy rice, don't fret—just throw it into a soup, and nobody will know any better. Coincidentally, rice is also an excellent way to bulk up a soup that you've added too much salt to.

What to Do with Day-Old, Hard Bread

A lady at the store who was standing in line behind me was complaining that the French bread she bought from there (because they don't add weird dough conditioners and preservatives) would always go hard in a day. She wondered aloud what to do about it if you don't need breadcrumbs. I grinned because I'd used this trick to revive killed bread before.

Take the loaf of bread, and wrap it in a damp towel. Leave it in the fridge overnight. The next day, unwrap the towel, and preheat the oven to 350° F. Lightly mist the surface of the bread with some water. Put the bread in the oven for 5 to 10 minutes. The steam from the water will reconstitute the bread.

V

Substitutions & Explanations

I've heard a lot of "Dino, I don't have _____, so can I try something else please?" I want to encourage that. It all flows into the Dino Philosophy of making recipes your own. Go right ahead and make the substitutions to make foods suit your kitchen and your budget. I'll also be including notes for certain ingredients, so that those who are about to use them use the right one. So here we go.

Asafetida: No substitute. Use good-quality sesame oil to compensate for the flavor difference. Asafetida has been described as one of the most vile-smelling things on the planet, and I would almost concur but for the fact that I love it so much. It's an integral part of my childhood smell memories, and I can't imagine South Indian food without it. For those who have kids, I'll make an analogy to Pokémon. When Ash was in the perfume city, they used essence of Vileplume to make their more distinct scents. That little bit of nasty smell made the final product smell divine. Similarly, even though asafetida by itself is quite rank, you don't smell it in the final dish if you use it properly.

Chiles: Use Thai bird chiles. They're hot and have multiple levels of heat inside the chile itself. If you can't get them, use jalapeño or serrano. Experiment with different types to see what you like. If you need something milder, go for a banana pepper. If you want something hotter, increase the amount of Thai bird chiles.

Do not use Scotch bonnet or habañero chiles in Indian food. Save them for the more Latin American-inspired dishes. The comment that chiles have flavor always greatly amused my less heat-inclined friends, but they do have flavor. They each have unique characteristics that blend with your foods in different ways.

If you want a milder chile experience, chances are that your skin is sensitive to them too. Let's not risk it. Pop on a pair of those food

23

service gloves before you get started Cut the chile in half lengthwise. With the tip of your knife's blade, scrape away the seeds and the inside membranes of the chile. If you're afraid of demolishing a chile, you can practice the technique on a bell pepper. Its seeds come in a neat package, and its membranes are large and easy to see.

If you dislike hot food in general, or your stomach is sensitive, try using a small amount of black pepper and work your way up as your tolerance increases.

Cilantro: I've sometimes heard people describe cilantro as having a soapy taste to it. I have no idea what they're talking about, but in the interest of helping people, I'll see what I can come up with. Italian flat-leaf parsley has a milder taste in comparison to its curly cousin. You should be able to get away with Italian parsley in most applications, although in Mexican foods, it won't taste quite as authentic. Does that mean you grin and bear a taste you don't like? Never! Have I taught you nothing? You make it the way you like it, and if people complain, they can get their food elsewhere.

Curry Leaves: No substitutes, unfortunately. Curry leaves have this earthy, smoky flavor that you cannot replicate with any other herb or spice combination. They grow in a tropical climate, which probably explains why I've got trees of them growing in my yard. Typically, fresh curry leaves should be torn up and tossed in hot oil, while dried curry leaves should be ground up and then added with any other spices.

Herbs: When using fresh herbs, add them at the end. When using dried, add with aromatics. The reason for this is because the different forms of herbs have different purposes. A dried herb needs to be added at the beginning, so that the flavors have time to leak into the rest of the dish. If they don't have enough time, they'll overpower the dish and stand out too much. You want dried ingredients to cook down as much as you can.

Fresh herbs, on the other hand, are added at the end to round out whatever flavors you have already developed. They're a bright, vivid addition to a dish, and having little bursts of fresh herbs on your tongue gives the dish a little "something else" that you wouldn't quite find with dried. Nobody is going to convince me that the light minty taste that fresh basil contains is preserved in the dried version. This doesn't mean that one is better than the other, but more so that each has its own purpose.

If you can't afford to have a large variety of oils on hand, a clean and simple canola or corn oil is a good multi-purpose oil for most dishes.

Oil: Use regular vegetable oil, unless specified. For frying, use peanut oil. For sautéing, a good corn oil is fine. Try to avoid olive oil for Asian dishes. Try to avoid sesame oil for Mediterranean dishes. Nothing tastes weirder than a long-simmered tomato sauce with a sesame oil taste. If you can't afford to have a large variety of oils on hand, a clean and simple canola or corn oil is a good multipurpose oil for most dishes. I am partial to peanut oil myself, but that is just because it gives a buttery taste when I make popcorn.

Oil, None desired: When using the recipes from this book that require oil (such as dressings, sauces, gravies) please use the full fat indicated. When the recipe asks you to pop some spices in oil, toss vegetables in oil, or otherwise use oil as a cooking medium, feel free to use a spray of nonstick cooking spray, or oil from an oil mister (my favorite brand is the Misto). This is because the oil is just there to convey the flavor of the spices to the rest of the food, and isn't necessarily providing too much in the way of texture.

Regardless of your reasons for avoiding oil, there are places where you won't miss the fat, and places where you will. If you're not sure, feel free to email me.

Oil, Olive: When cooking, go for regular olive oil. When using in dressings, dips, or uncooked, use extra virgin. *Do not touch light olive oil*, as it's basically a marketing ploy to palm off cheap oil that's got no flavor. The method for getting good quality olive oil is called "cold pressing," and it involves some fairly expensive machines to slowly press out the oil from the olives. Good extra virgin olive oil is obtained from the "first pressing," which means that the olives haven't been tinkered with before they met with the machine.

It has a floral, green aroma, and the taste is light and delicate. Extra virgin olive oil is sensitive to heat and light, which is why many come in dark colored bottles. White truffle oil, which is sort of like a cousin of olive oil, is olive oil that's been steeped with truffles. Truffles are expensive, so it's often cheaper for the home cook to snag a $20

bottle of truffle oil than shell out $50 an ounce for truffles.

Oil, Sesame: Do not touch toasted sesame oil for Indian dishes. Use toasted only for the stuff like Japanese, Chinese, Thai, and Vietnamese dishes. The flavor would be overpowering to the spices, and the final dish will taste off to anyone who's eaten Indian food before. Besides that, toasted sesame oil can get pretty pricey. Save it for dishes where you can use it uncooked, and where its subtle undertones have a chance to play. Try it drizzled onto cucumber slices with a little lemon. For cooking, use regular sesame oil. If you can find it, get what's called "gingelly" or "til" oil at the local Indian store for an authentic Indian food flavor.

Pickles: An Indian pickle is nothing like its similarly-named western counterpart. It's something that's been preserved in spices, salt, and oil, not vinegar. They generally involve large amounts of salt and chiles, although milder pickles are quite common. Use them *very* sparingly, as they are meant to be enhancements to flavor, not an actual dish. Never use more than 1 teaspoon on your plate to accompany your meal. I have included a pickle recipe (Mango Relish, page 82) in this book, so feel free to experiment.

Potatoes: If you don't like, eat, or have potatoes, you are welcome to use any starchy vegetable in its place, in situations where you're keeping the potatoes in cubes. For example, in the Indian Roasted Potatoes (page 68), you can use plantains, sweet potatoes, parsnips, turnips, or any other starchy vegetable, and you'll be fine. The only situation I would discourage you from substituting in this manner are with things where the mashed potatoes give the final dish its final texture, such as Herb-Crusted Potato Patties (page 63), Flautas (page 88), or Omusubi (page 85). In these cases, you need for the vegetable to behave exactly like a mashed potato would.

Spices: Use whole, unless powder is specified. If substituting a ground spice, use half the amount, and add with your aromatics (onions, peppers, garlic, etc.). The reason to avoid ground spices if you can help it is that as soon as you grind a spice, it begins to lose its potency and the more complex undertones. Someone who dislikes a particular spice blend most likely dislikes it because eating already-ground spices is akin to carving Michelangelo's David with a hammer and a spatula—it can be done, but the results won't be the same. Like the example, you would miss out on the subtle details that the spice has. Freshly ground black pepper is not only hot, but it's also slightly smoky and a little bit earthy. Similarly, freshly pounded coriander seeds have a mildly sweet smell to them. Cumin, when it is used whole and popped in oil, has the same smokiness we all know it for, but it also has a distinctly nutty smell too. There is no comparison between ground and whole cumin. With the exception of cinnamon, it's best to get whole spices, and grind them down yourself.

If you do use powders, make sure to have them in airtight containers. This means that you might have to change the container that the spice is bottled in, but that's fine. The containers they sell spices in are there to attract your eye, and make you want to buy them. They are not suitable for storing the spices. Unless you're in need of fresh spices every week, get some airtight containers for your spices. It's worth the few cents you would spend on the boxes.

V

Deciphering the Time/Serving Size Glyphs:

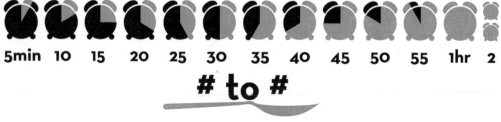

5min   10   15   20   25   30   35   40   45   50   55   1hr   2

to

SERVING SIZE

Chapter 1:
Meals in One Pot

The following dishes are what I would consider to be meals all by themselves. It's not the traditional "American" meal per se, but I would be quite full after eating a bowl. In my opinion, these are also among the easiest to customize. If you're a beginning cook, make sure to read through the section on cooking techniques. Once you've finished that, you're more or less ready to try these.

There's more "wiggle room" in these dishes than you would have in a dish that requires stacks of ingredients. What do you need to complete the one-pot meal? Usually, some rice in the bottom of your bowl will make the meal totally complete. These are the sorts of things that I pack for my lunch when I'm headed out to work and the like.

Because they're so customizable, these are the dishes that I'd like you to try first. Try the variations, or even make up your own and give those a shot. These are so easy to make yours that your friends will get used to your versions of things and wouldn't ever suspect that you could have creatively borrowed the recipe from someone else!

V

That One Soup Dino Makes

As you, my lovely readers, know well, I am capable of a variety of soups and stews. However, I sometimes get a request for "that one soup like how Dino makes." Aside from being grammatically cringe-worthy, it's also highly useless when trying to describe what the soup is, what goes in it, or much of anything else. All you know is that it's good, because it's my recipe.

That's the point of this recipe. It's a sort of default soup for when you don't really know what you're in the mood to eat, or are going to feed a person used to eating milk or meat (the creamy texture and the smoky flavors help this to happen). The vegetables here are fairly neutral and don't really bring in too much flavor. This is essentially what I like to call a "mother soup" (much like the "mother sauces" found in European cuisine), because you're supposed to add stuff to it. It tastes lovely all by itself but leaves something to be desired in terms of variety.

Make this soup your own by adding your favorite blends of frozen vegetables, favorite quick-cooking greens such as spinach or arugula, or your favorite canned vegetables or beans. The base flavors took a while to lay down, so you can play fast and loose with the other ingredients.

You can also take it totally gourmet and add roasted butternut squash, roasted red peppers, caramelized onions, garden fresh herbs, sun-dried tomatoes, olives, marinated artichoke hearts, or whatever you can think of. How about some morel, shiitake, oyster, crimini, and cloud ear mushrooms? Maybe some black beans, avocado, huitlacoche, and fresh tomato for a Tex-Mex-like thing. You can make the final product as fancy or plain as you'd like. This is a concentrated soup, meant to be ready for storage. A lot of the water has boiled off, and the final product will seem like it's fatty. That's normal.

 **10 to 15**

Ingredients:

- 2 tablespoons oil
- 1/2 tablespoon (either yellow or black) mustard seeds
- 1 tablespoon cumin seeds
- 1 tablespoon coriander seeds, lightly crushed
- 1 large onion, chopped fine
- 2 teaspoons turmeric
- 1 tablespoon salt
- 2 bay leaves
- 6 potatoes, roughly chopped

- 5 small summer squash, chopped
- 1 pound carrots, scrubbed and chopped
- Small bunch watercress
- Small bunch Italian parsley
- Up to 6 cups water
- 2 cans coconut milk
- Any other ingredients you're adding (precooked)

Dino Sarma Weierman | Alternative Vegan

Instructions:

This soup starts off in layers and builds up step by step. Start by dicing your onion. Then heat the oil in a large stockpot on high heat. When the oil is hot, pour in the mustard seeds. When they pop and crackle, add the cumin. When you can smell a strong cumin smell, and the cumin is popping, add the crushed coriander seeds. Wait about 10 seconds and add the onions. Stir immediately to coat in the oil. Sprinkle in the salt and turmeric, and add both bay leaves. Stir until the onions are all yellow.

Reduce the heat to medium-low and put on the lid. You want it to cook for about 15 minutes, covered, to slowly sweat. Every 5 minutes, come back and stir the onions to redistribute the spices. While the onions are sweating, chop the carrots. If you have time, start in on the potatoes as well. Check the onions at the end of the 15 minutes. If they're completely softened, increase the heat to high. Stir the onions until evenly coated in the oil. Add the potatoes and carrots. If you still have more potatoes to chop, don't worry about it—we can add those as soon as they're chopped. Stir the vegetables to coat evenly in the oil and the spices. Reduce the heat to low and cover. Finish chopping your potatoes and add them to the pot as you complete them. Let the potatoes cook in the pot dry for 15 to 20 minutes.

While the potatoes are cooking, chop the watercress, parsley, and squash. At the end of 15 minutes, open up the lid of the pot, and pour in just enough water to barely cover the vegetables. Allow the water to come to a full boil. Turn down the heat to a simmer, and allow the soup to simmer, covered, an additional 5 minutes. You may stop the soup at this point and freeze it. Then, later on, when ready to serve, you would reheat the soup to come back to a simmer.

Open the lid and layer on the squash, watercress, parsley, and coconut milk (in that order) and *do not stir*. Just let it sit like that in layers and cover the lid. Let it sit for 10 minutes, at a low simmer, covered. At the end of the 10 minutes, the soup will be ready for any other vegetables you'll be adding to dress this up. After the addition of any such ingredients, make sure to let the soup come together in a medium boil for about 5 minutes before serving.

Serve with a side of beans and a green salad. Have plenty of croutons ready to grab.

Uppuma

Uppuma is a South Indian dish that uses a wheat product called sooji (in Hindi). In the United States, most people wouldn't know what you're talking about, so I've found that farina (AKA cream of wheat) works perfectly well. This recipe isn't as tricky as it seems, because you develop a knack for it once you've made it a couple of times. Figure on the texture of the stuff in the pot being a little bit wetter than couscous. You don't want it to be too wet like porridge. You want it to finish on the dry side.

 6

Ingredients:

- ▶ 2 cups sooji or farina
- ▶ 2 tablespoons oil
- ▶ 1 teaspoon mustard seeds
- ▶ 1 teaspoon cumin seeds
- ▶ 1/8 teaspoon asafetida (optional)
- ▶ Handful curry leaves (optional)
- ▶ 1 large onion, diced
- ▶ 1/4 teaspoon turmeric
- ▶ Salt
- ▶ 1/4 cup diced carrots
- ▶ 1/4 cup corn
- ▶ 1/4 cup green peas
- ▶ 1 1/2 cups water plus 1 cup water
- ▶ 1 chile, minced

What is cumin?

Cumin is a brown seed that grows well in tropical climates. Its smoky, pungent aroma adds a distinct flavor that cannot be replicated by any other spice.

It is popular in Latin American and Asian cuisines. It is especially common in Indian cuisine, where it can be found in everything from the fiery curries of the North to the quiet soups of the South.

Instructions:

Pour the sooji into a skillet and roast over a gentle flame. You want the stove at medium-low to medium so that you don't burn the sooji. The reason for roasting is that it enhances the dimensions of flavor. It's also the only way I know how to make the stuff, because that's how my mother taught me, and I'm not comfortable with trying to use unroasted sooji.

Make sure you constantly stir the sooji to avoid burning, and reduce the flame if you notice any smoke coming from the pan. This should take anywhere from 10 to 15 minutes. When the sooji smells lightly nutty and looks a tan color, remove it from the heat and pour it into a bowl to cool. Rinse out your pan and place it over high heat.

When the water evaporates, pour in the oil and wait for it to heat. Add the mustard seeds. In about 30 seconds, they should be exploding. Add the cumin seeds. They should be popping before long. Add the asafetida and wait 5 seconds for it to sizzle. Tear the curry leaves in half, add them to the skillet, and step back, because they will explode! Immediately add the chile and onions. Generously sprinkle in salt to taste and the turmeric.

Stir the onions around the pan to combine with the oil and the turmeric. When all the pieces are yellow, you've combined enough. Let the onions get softened but not browned. When the onions are soft, add the carrots and corn. Stir to combine all the ingredients. When the carrots are soft, add the peas. Stir everything to evenly coat all the vegetables with the oil and spices.

Pour in the 1 1/2 cups water. It should come to a full boil quickly. Start stirring everything together, and make sure to scrape the bottom of the pan to release any particles stuck there.

While constantly stirring the ingredients in the liquid in the pan, pour the roasted sooji into the pan in a steady stream. If you can't stir and pour simultaneously, ask for help. Everything should start coming together quickly. If it looks too dry, add a little bit more water, until it's at the consistency of thick porridge. Keep stirring until the excess water evaporates and you're left with a dry final product.

This is a stand-alone meal, because it has everything you'll need in one bowl!

Basic Kale Soup

Make sure to try some of the variations. This soup is bland on its own and needs some sidebar vegetables in there to make it interesting. If you prefer the milder flavors, you may stick to the basic recipe, but I would recommend at least trying one or two variations to avoid making the same thing all the time.

 4 to 6

Ingredients:

▶ 1 tablespoon oil

▶ 1 teaspoon cumin seeds

▶ 1 large onion, finely minced

▶ Salt

▶ 1 clove garlic, minced

▶ 1 teaspoon freshly ground black pepper

▶ 1 head kale, sliced, and stems diced

▶ 4 cups water

▶ 1 cup minced parsley

Instructions:

Add oil to the bottom of a large heavy-bottomed pot. Turn on the stove to high heat. When the oil is hot, add your cumin seeds. In about a minute, if you made sure to get the oil good and hot, you'll have the cumin seeds popping and cracking. At this moment, add your onions. Sprinkle in salt to taste. Stir to evenly coat in the oil. Cook for about 5 minutes, or until soft.

Add the garlic, pepper, and chopped kale, and stir into the onion mixture so that the pieces of kale are evenly coated in the oil. You may have to add the kale in batches if your pot isn't that large. Add a batch, stir it around, and wait for it to wilt down. When there's more room, add subsequent batches and continue to stir and wilt the kale. Sprinkle on salt. Toss through over the heat for about 5 minutes. Add the water. Bring it to a full boil, and then reduce to a simmer. Allow it to cook for about 20 minutes. When cooked, sprinkle in parsley and let sit about 5 minutes.

Variations:

1 pound diced, cooked potato, stirred in at the end; 8 ounces mushrooms, sliced, added in 10 minutes before removing from heat; 1 head of cabbage, sliced, added in 10 minutes before finishing; 1 pound zucchini, cut in half lengthwise and sliced into half-moons, added in roughly 5 minutes before removing from heat; Chile oil, added in right at the end of cooking. Add a teaspoon or so to each bowl of soup; 1 tablespoon kimchee; 1 pound cooked chickpeas added in the last 10 minutes of cooking; or 1 pound cooked kidney beans added in the last 5 minutes of cooking.

Combine all the variations to make a very filling soup

Butternut Squash

This squash is not only mindlessly easy to make but pulses to make a creamy, rich, decadent soup. I'm including multiple variations, because I love the stuff, and I'd like to get people to at least try it. Because it stands alone (for the most part) you can use this soup as an appetizer before starting the rest of your meal. In the winter it is more difficult to find fresh herbs in your garden, so I made this recipe using dried herbs. However, because you don't have a chance to chop the thyme and rosemary to release the oils properly, gently rub them between the palms of your hands before adding them to the dish. You should smell them once you start breaking them up.

 4

Ingredients:

- ▶ 1 medium butternut squash
- ▶ 2 cups vegetable stock
- ▶ 1/2 teaspoon dried sage, or 1 teaspoon fresh
- ▶ 1 teaspoon dried rosemary, crushed gently between your palms
- ▶ 1/2 teaspoon dried thyme, crushed gently between your palms

Instructions:

The easiest way to peel squash for soup (in my opinion) is to microwave it. Cut the squash into large chunks (roughly split it into eight pieces), and put it in a microwave-safe bowl with 1/4 cup of water. Cover loosely with a plastic lid. Nuke it until the squash is tender (it takes my microwave about 15 minutes). Now, you should be able to easily scoop out the seeds and flesh with a spoon. Scoop out the flesh of the squash and simmer over medium-low heat with the stock and herbs for about 10 minutes. Remove from the heat and blend until smooth.

Variations:

For a smoother texture, strain through a sieve before serving it piping hot with a side of croutons.

For those like myself who like some heat in their food, add in a red chile or two before simmering and blend it along with the squash. (I find Tabasco sauce to have an offensive flavor with butternut squash.)

If you want your soup thicker, stir in a little bit of hummus.

If you like it a little sweeter, add some carrots to the microwave with your squash.

If you want extra protein in it, add 1/4 pound of cooked red lentils to the blender along with the squash.

To make it a dressing, take 1/2 cup of the soup, 1/4 cup olive oil, and 1/4 cup of balsamic vinegar, and whisk vigorously. Then stir in some fresh dill, parsley, and basil for a really nice zip.

Quick Chickpea Soup

I've made this recipe with precooked beans (the giant lot I make on weekends), which is the reason I'm asking you to use canned beans. Cooking your own is always best, but we're looking for speed here. The key is finding the balance of tomato to chickpeas. You can use larger or smaller cans as you wish, but make sure to adjust the flavorings. I've gotten feedback from my readers about this particular dish. The overwhelming consensus is that the soup really is freakishly fast to throw together and that they sincerely wished they'd increased the amount. I'm not saying that you'll necessarily need to double the recipe. If you want to, I won't tell anyone.

 4

Ingredients:

- 1 teaspoon canola, peanut, or safflower oil (can take high temps)
- 1/4 teaspoon cumin seeds
- 1/2 teaspoon sesame seeds
- 3 stalks curry leaves, if available
- 1 medium onion, chopped
- 1/4 teaspoon turmeric
- Salt
- 1 pound canned tomato, drained
- 1 pound canned chickpeas, drained
- 1 1/2 cups water
- Fresh chiles, chopped

Instructions:

Heat oil over high heat in a wide, shallow pan. Sprinkle in cumin. When you hear the cumin popping (about 30 seconds, if the oil is hot), add in sesame seeds. When the sesame seeds brown, strip the curry leaves off their stalks, tear them in half, and toss them in along with the onion. Reduce the heat to medium-high, and sprinkle in turmeric and a little bit of salt. Sauté onions until soft (about 1 minute). Bring the heat back to high and add in the can of tomatoes. Stir vigorously for about 3 to 5 minutes. You'll see the tomatoes breaking down a little—this is a good thing. Add the chickpeas. When the beans are coated with the tomatoes, add the water. Add chopped-up chiles to taste. When water comes to a boil, you're done!

Serve all by itself, over brown rice, or with your favorite short pasta or Asian-style noodles. Adding in the grains will make it so that you have a complete meal in one bowl.

Variations:

For a creamier soup: **Strain some of the beans from the soup at the end, and blend them in a blender with a little bit of the soup water. Or add 1 tablespoon tahini at the end and stir through.**

For heartier soup: **Add a pound of frozen vegetables along with the chickpeas.**

After the onions soften, add 2 tablespoons of tomato paste and cook for a minute or two. If you notice a tinny flavor in the tomatoes from the can, add 1/2 capful of vanilla extract when you add in the tomatoes. This goes for paste, purée, or pieces of tomato from a can.

Green Leafy Soup

Freezes beautifully, so I'm giving large proportions. A lot of people like to remove the stalks, and you may do so if you want, but it's best to just cut up the leaves with the stalks on. You'd cut the rougher portions really finely but chop the parts of the leaves without stalks in bigger pieces, and everything will get cooked at the same time. Your local grocery store may have premixed, prewashed, precut greens that come in a bag. These are perfectly acceptable as long as they still look fresh and green.

 10

Ingredients:

- ▶ 1 pound kale
- ▶ 1 pound collard greens
- ▶ 1 pound mustard greens
- ▶ 2 tablespoons olive oil
- ▶ 1 large white onion, finely diced
- ▶ 1 large red onion, finely diced
- ▶ 1 head garlic, finely minced
- ▶ 1 teaspoon salt
- ▶ 1 tablespoon red pepper flakes
- ▶ 1 teaspoon freshly ground black pepper
- ▶ 1 1/2 cups stock
- ▶ 2 cups coconut milk
- ▶ 1 1/2 cups water
- ▶ Salt

Instructions:

Chop your greens to bite-sized pieces. Finely chop the stems and treat them like you would the leaves. Heat the olive oil in the stock pot. When the oil gets hot, add the onions and the garlic, and sauté until softened. Add the chopped greens, and sprinkle with salt to leach the water out. Stir the greens around in the aromatics to get them coated, roughly 10 minutes. You will likely have to add the greens in waves, let them cook down a bit to make some more space, and add the next batch. Add in the red pepper flakes and black pepper, and stir an additional 5 minutes. Pour in the stock, and cover with the lid.

When the soup comes to a full boil, reduce to a simmer, and let the greens simmer, not boil, for about 1 hour (now you know why boiled greens taste like shit—they're boiled). About 10 minutes before removing from the heat, stir in the coconut milk. If the soup looks too thick to you, or too creamy, add some water until it gets to the desired thickness. This is when you want to taste the soup. If it's not salty enough, not hot enough, or needs something more, this is where you'd do that. In between additions of pepper flakes, you're going to have to let them cook for a few minutes to get integrated in the soup.

Serve hot, by itself or over brown rice. Offer wedges of lime to each diner when serving.

If you would prefer other vegetables in this soup, you can add potatoes, pumpkin, green beans, carrots, cabbage, spinach, parsnips, winter melon, or artichoke hearts without disturbing what's already there. Believe me, that amount of green leafy vegetables can take it. You may scale this down if you cannot acquire that many greens, or if you prefer to make a smaller quantity.

Venn Pongal

During the month of Thai (usually hits in early January) in Tamil Nadu, the women dress themselves up in bright yellow saris (with red borders, of course), get the house sparkling clean, and begin cooking up savory pots of rice stew, called pongal. (There is also a "chakkarai," or sweet pongal, but I don't care for it.) These three days, the harvest festival of Pongal is celebrated. (Incidentally, this is how you can tell whether I'm talking about the dish or the celebration—the celebration is capitalized.)

To symbolize the harvest, families find all their old, worn-out clothing, and create a large bonfire in which to burn the clothes. The father gives his family and servants new clothes, money, and other gifts. This also marks the time for old, unclean thoughts to be scrubbed out of the mind, and for new, spiritual thoughts to enter. It's a time of mental and physical renewal and is celebrated with equal exuberance across the caste and religious lines.

Which oil should I use?

In applications where the flavor of the oil is not important, such as highly spiced cooked dishes, stick with a neutral-flavored oil, like safflower, corn, vegetable, peanut, or sunflower. For dressings and sauces where you can taste the oil, use the specified oil, such as sesame or olive. Beyond the issue of the flavor of the oil being masked comes the issue of the spices being masked, as well. It is always best to use the oil(s) suggested.

In the north, it's known as kichdi, but as we all know, nobody north of Chennai knows the first thing about pongal! They add weird things in there, like cloves or cardamom. Ew. Take it from someone who is from the Indian south: you cannot find a decent pongal unless it's made properly. The main flavor components of a good pongal are the cumin, the black pepper, and the ginger. The curry leaves and asafetida help, but the stars here are the three I just described.

If a south Indian can afford nuts, she will use them. This means that if cashews are a little out of your price range, leave them out. They're not integral, but they certainly add a nice contrast to the mushy consistency of the rice. That's the other main thing to remember about pongal: it needs to be mushy. If you have to chew it too long, aside from the cashews, you haven't cooked it long enough. This is the type of thing given to young children (without the nuts) and older people. People of all ages enjoy pongal.

My mother, being the kitchen innovator that she is, would always make the stuff in a rice cooker, because it's easier to just dump everything in and forget about it. To be honest, I do the same thing. When you don't want to be bothered with keeping track of...stuff, just dump everything in a pot, and pretend it doesn't exist until everything is cooked through. Then just season the food and serve it however you like.

The reason I use two separate pots for the rice/daal and the spices is mainly because of my mother's trick with working everything in a rice cooker. You could technically do the spices in oil, add the rice and daal to the spices, and then add the water. I don't know if it would taste the same, though. Either way, I like pongal quite a lot.

4

Ingredients:

- ▶ 1 cup white or brown long-grain (not basmati) rice
- ▶ 1/2 cup moong daal (or yellow split peas)
- ▶ 1 teaspoon turmeric
- ▶ 1 tablespoon freshly ground black pepper
- ▶ 6 cups water
- ▶ Salt
- ▶ 2 tablespoons oil
- ▶ 1 teaspoon mustard seeds
- ▶ 1 teaspoon cumin seed
- ▶ 1/8 teaspoon asafetida
- ▶ 15 stalks curry leaves
- ▶ 1/4 cup of cashews
- ▶ 1 tablespoon grated ginger

Instructions:

In a large pot, boil the rice, daal, turmeric, and ground black pepper in the water until the rice and daal both reach the consistency of thick oatmeal. Don't be fooled into thinking it's done if the rice just pretends to be mushy enough. This stuff needs to be mushy. On my stove, this took around 40 minutes at a medium simmer.

If you're nervous about the daal getting cooked, feel free to cook it in the water until it's soft first. Then add the rice, turmeric, and black pepper along with extra water (to replace what's evaporated) and cook it down until the rice is mushy. This will take slightly longer because you're waiting for both things to cook completely, but it does more or less guarantee that the daal will be soft enough. Add a little less salt than you think you need to your liking after the rice and daal are cooked through.

Don't use basmati for this dish as it requires sturdy rice that can stand up to the hard boiling you're going to give it. I know that the rice smells good already—that's the point! It's supposed to be tempting you far before it's anywhere near complete.

When the rice and daal are cooked, start preparing the seasoning. It takes just under 2 minutes, so you can't have it prepared ahead of time.

In a small saucepan, heat the oil until a small wisp of smoke comes out of the top. Add the mustard seeds and wait about 30 seconds for them to pop. When the popping has subsided a bit, add the cumin seeds and asafetida. Wait another 30 seconds for the cumin seeds to pop. The seeds will turn a darker brown. Strip the curry leaves off their stalks, tear them in half, and add them. Immediately after the curry leaves explode, add the cashews and ginger. Stir the cashews continually until the nuts become lightly toasted.

Pour in about a cup of the rice and daal mixture and stir. I think we do this step to ensure that we get every last drop of oil and spice into the rice pot again, but I mainly do it because that's what my mother did. Wash out the spice pot with some water, and pour the spiced water into the rice pot.

Stir the rice, daal, and spices until they're fully combined. Allow the spices and rice and daal to cook in the pot over medium heat for another 15 to 30 minutes for everything to get combined.

Taste for salt and heat. If it's too bland, add some extra ground black pepper or grated ginger. Make sure there's enough salt, because you want everything incorporated when it's hot.

Erissery (Avial, Kootu)

Thousands of years ago, in Kerala, there was a great asura (demon) king named Mahabali. Although he was from the race of demons, he was a just and kind king. So kind was he that any person who stood before him to make a request immediately got what he wanted. His people were happy, and Mahabali loved them with all of his heart.

One day, the god Vishnu in the guise of a small beggar came to Mahabali and asked for a request. Being the loving king that he was, Mahabali wanted to know what that request was. Vishnu said, "I want enough land to put three [of my] feet on." Mahabali laughed, and immediately told the little beggar that the request would be happily granted.

Suddenly, Vishnu began to grow, and grow, and grow. He grew to his full, massive size. With one foot, he covered all of the Earth. With another foot, he covered all of the skies. Vishnu then looked down at Mahabali, and said, "I still need one more foot's space." Mahabali offered his head as the third foot's space.

Vishnu, touched by how humble the good king was, revealed his identity as a god. He granted Mahabali any boon that his heart desired. Mahabali loved his people so much that he only asked that he be allowed to return to visit them once a year. For 10 days around August or September (Indians use a lunar calendar), the festival of Onam is celebrated.

Keralites the world over celebrate this harvest festival with plantain chips, stewed vegetables, and a lot of coconut. This particular dish showcases the love that the region of Kerala (in the south of India) has for its coconuts. Women and men use the oil on their hair and skin. The food is bursting with coconut. Everything from sweet to salty to tasty has lots of the delicate snowflakes of coconut in it. It must work because Malayali women don't have grey hair until very old age, and both men and women don't get wrinkles until they reach their twilight years.

This particular dish should be served piping hot over rice. Make sure to have enough of it for second and third helpings, because it will go rather quickly.

 **6 to 10**

Ingredients:

▶ 1 tablespoon oil

▶ 1 tablespoon mustard seeds

▶ 15 stalks curry leaves, if available

▶ 1 pound black-eyed peas, soaked overnight

▶ 3 quarts water plus an additional 3 quarts

▶ 1 teaspoon turmeric

▶ 1 pound yellow squash

▶ 1/2 cup grated coconut (dried or fresh)

▶ 1 tablespoon cumin seeds

▶ 3 dried chiles

▶ Salt and freshly ground black pepper

Instructions:

In a heavy-bottomed stockpot, heat the oil over high heat until a small wisp of smoke escapes the surface. Add the mustard seeds and wait for about 30 seconds for the seeds to pop. Strip the curry leaves off their stalks, tear them in half, and add them. Immediately add the black-eyed peas and about 3 quarts of the water. Reserve the other 3 quarts to add in case you need more later. Add the turmeric and stir the beans and spices to combine. You will boil these, covered, for 45 to 60 minutes.

While the water comes to a boil, slice the squash in half lengthwise. Slice the halves in half lengthwise again. You should be left with four squash sticks. Cut the sticks (width-wise this time) into 1/2-inch pieces. Set them aside.

In a skillet, combine the grated coconut, the cumin, and the dried chiles. Gently toast them over a medium flame until you smell the aroma of the cumin seeds intertwined with the lightly-browned roasted coconut. The coconut will become a light woodsy brown. That's the perfect color.

Once the spices and coconut are roasted to perfection, pour them all into the jar of a blender with about 3 cups of water. The roasted coconut and roasted spices will release some of their flavors into the water in the blender. Add a generous dose of salt (you can adjust later, as needed). Blend on high speed until everything is ground down. You'll never get it down to a paste, but you can get the coconut finely ground. This will also work if you cheated and didn't manage to get the coconut finely ground the first time around. This definitely is a good thing if you used the fresh coconut.

At this point, the water in the pot that's cooking the beans should have reduced considerably. About 40 minutes into the bean boiling, check one of the beans and see if it's getting cooked. If it's almost there, you're ready to add the squash. If it's still not quite there, get a glass of water and relax until the beans are cooked through, because you're most likely sweating a little bit by now.

After 45 to 60 minutes, depending on your stove, the beans should be mostly cooked through. Add the squash, and boil for another 10 minutes. Add the coconut spice paste and reduce the heat to a simmer. Stir everything to combine all the ingredients, and simmer for another 10 minutes.

Test the Erissery for salt. If there isn't enough, add enough to suit you. Just be careful not to over-salt the food!

Serve the Erissery over hot white or brown rice. It's perfect as a meal in one pot. Always have plenty of fiery hot pickles (see page 84) on the side, as some diners may want things hotter than the few scant chiles we've added to this dish. Have plenty of icy-cold water and cold shredded cucumber tossed with lemon juice at the ready for those whose tongues need blander flavors.

Chipotle Garlic Risotto

Risotto is a dish that should have been vegan to begin with. The texture of the rice and the flavor of your stock should be more than ample to get your taste buds dancing and your tongue begging for more. Adding nonvegan ingredients to risotto just dilutes out those experiences and overpowers the delicate little rice grains. Use this recipe, but suit it to your own tastes. If you don't like hot foods, then use roasted red peppers instead of chipotle peppers.

Why arborio?

For most rice dishes, a nice long-grain rice should do just fine. In certain rice dishes, like risotto, you're looking for a particular texture and starch content. Arborio rice is a short-grain rice with a lot of starch. These starches are liberated from the surface of the rice when the rice is stirred. The grains rub against each other and release their starches into the surrounding liquid. It wouldn't quite work with regular long-grain rice.

The chipotle is actually just a jalapeño pepper that's been smoked and dried. Chipotles in adobo are the chipotle chiles sitting in a spicy sauce. It's a unique flavor, and I would recommend it to anyone who hasn't ventured into Mexican cuisine very often.

The sort of "Rolls Royce" of risotto (to quote Mario Batali) is arborio rice. It's a short-grain Italian rice that works beautifully with a good vegetable stock and crisp white wine. I suggest using a pinot grigio, because an Italian wine will marry well with the arborio and it won't overpower anything. You do have a lot of discretion, however. Don't use a sweet white wine, like gewürztraminer, because it'll just taste weird at the end. If you don't like having alcohol in the house, just use stock. It'll still be fine.

Stirring is what develops the starches in the risotto, so don't skimp on it! If your arms are prone to getting tired, you can cheat and invite all your friends for a "risotto party" and say that everyone gets a turn at stirring the risotto. Then you can pretend to be this wicked creative host, and have out a bunch of different ingredients out, so that people can customize their own individual bowls of risotto. Have many rolls of crusty bread, oil with some fresh herbs and salt (I like a mix of basil and oregano), and a couple of bottles of the wine to use in your risotto. You'll have them talking about that party for years!

If you want to, you can serve little accompaniments like roasted vegetables, fresh tomatoes, sliced red onions, or any other side dish you deem to be a contrast to the rich creamy risotto. I like to give my guests a choice in their risotto toppings. Try having sautéed mushrooms, interesting olives (without pits), cherry tomatoes tossed in lemon juice, field greens salad, and different kinds of nuts. People will have fun building their own individual risottos.

The addition of chipotle and cumin to risotto is my little nod to that fusion cuisine thing everyone is so excited about. You can leave them out if you want to, but you'd be missing out.

4 to 6

Ingredients:

- 2 tablespoons olive oil
- 2 cups arborio rice
- 1 clove garlic, minced
- 1 scant teaspoon cumin
- 4 cups vegetable stock (low-sodium), simmering
- 4 cups pinot grigio, at room temperature, poured into a bowl
- 4 cups water, simmering
- 1 chipotle in adobo, finely minced
- Salt

Instructions:

Start with a wide skillet. A paella pan works for this just fine. Heat the olive oil over medium-high heat. When it gets hot, pour in your rice and garlic and stir well to combine.

Continue to stir the rice until you see it getting a little puffed-looking and it smells nutty. It might get a little bit browner in color, which is a good thing. Add your cumin powder, and stir everything to combine. Pour in 2 cups of stock and 1 cup of wine. You can eyeball it, because this isn't like baking. A standard ladle is usually about a cup. Don't bother trying to avoid cross-contamination with the wine—you'll most likely end up using all the liquid and more.

Stir the rice around vigorously to get everything combined. As the rice begins to absorb the water, continue alternating

between the wine and the stock. You'll notice a sort of gravy forming around the rice, which is what we're looking for. Continue to stir.

It will continue to absorb the water, and the gravy will get thicker and thicker. This is also a good thing. Taste a grain of rice after about the third addition of wine or stock (by this point, I've had a few glasses from the other bottles of wine, so it's tough to keep track). If it's still not done, just keep alternating your stock and wine.

This is where the water comes in. Some people's stoves treat rice differently, and I find it best to have reserved water in dishes like this. Nothing is worse than ruining a whole pot of risotto at the eleventh hour. You may not need it, but having it will save angry phone calls to me. If you run out of the stock and wine, use water until the rice is cooked to your liking.

When the risotto is done, let it sit (if you can resist, that is) for about 5 minutes. Taste it for salt. If it's not salty enough, you can add more salt and stir it through. Because the stock should have had enough salt in it, I doubt that you'll need to. Being a salt fiend, I tend to have salt sitting on the table in any case.

When you're ready to serve it, arrange a neat little pile of the chipotle chiles on top and serve. This goes great with a fresh green salad, dressed with lemon juice and a lot of garlicky croutons. Serve it with a bottle of white wine to give the meal a nice rounded feeling.

Locro de Papa

While I was in the mountains in Quito, Ecuador, I stayed at a decidedly upscale hotel called La Ronda. The service was stellar and the people were friendly. That night, after going out to some clubs and coming back feeling a little drained, I wanted to order something from room service that was vegetarian and would calm my dancing stomach. Locro de papa: papas, aguacate, ajo—potatoes, avocado, garlic—all three of those words leapt off of the pages of the menu, and my mouth watered as I anticipated what was to come. I called down and ordered a bowl, with a side dish of garlic bread and a spinach salad. It arrived. I opened up the little brown crock, and the punchy garlic leapt out and greeted me. I tasted it. I was in heaven.

It was rich and creamy. My mouth savored the contrasting textures of the potatoes and the avocado. The garlic was just perfect—adding a gentle counterpoint to the smooth, creamy textures.

Traditional locro de papa contains both milk and butter. In my version, the roux mimics the texture and gives you a much lower fat version of the traditional butter- and milk-laden soup. It's so rich and delicious as a starter. However, the potatoes and avocado are so filling that it would work just fine as a main course. The avocado gives the soup a creamy texture that you cannot replicate with anything else.

If you're making this at home, please do not use too much else in the way of seasoning. The charm of this soup is its simplicity in flavor. I would personally prefer an even simpler mode of making the soup, but in my opinion this is a good primer for a beginning chef, as it combines a variety of basic techniques. I find recipes that are so simple to be a testament to a talented cook, because the ingredients must stand bare, without any major flavorings to hide behind.

⏰ 4 to 6

Ingredients:

- 3 cups water
- 5 small red new potatoes, diced into 1/2-inch cubes
- 1 small red onion, diced
- 1 clove of garlic, minced
- 1 tablespoon oil for the roux plus 1 tablespoon oil for sautéing
- 1 tablespoon flour
- 1 small hass avocado, thinly sliced
- Salt and freshly ground black pepper
- 4 to 6 leaves of cilantro (optional)

Instructions:

In a pot, let the water come to a boil. While the water is heating, chop the potatoes, onions, and garlic. In a skillet, heat one of the tablespoons of oil over medium-high heat. When the oil is hot, sprinkle in the flour and whisk or stir through to combine. When the roux has reached a light blond color, pour in 1 cup of water from the pot on the stove. Whisk vigorously to combine. Allow the liquid in your skillet to come to a full boil, then turn off the heat and set aside.

When the water comes to a full boil, drop in the potatoes.

In a separate skillet, pour in the second tablespoon of the oil. Sauté the garlic and onions until softened. When they are soft, add them to the pot of boiling water and potatoes. Add the "gravy" (oil, flour, and water mixture) to the pot as well, and stir to combine. When the potatoes are tender, remove from the heat. Add salt and pepper to your taste.

In each diner's bowl, pour in about 1/2 cup of soup. Lay 3 to 5 avocado slices on top of the soup. Garnish with a leaf of cilantro, if you like. If you're a garlic fiend, like me, finely mince a clove of garlic and stir into the soup in the last minute or two of cooking. You'll get a strong garlic flavor.

Green Split Pea Soup

I just put these things into a crock put and turned it on. What resulted was a thick, rich soup that tasted fantastic all by itself. I ordinarily loathe sweet potatoes, but this one made it possible for me to eat them. Unlike regular potatoes, sweet potatoes don't get gummy when you grind them in the blender. The split peas control the gummy texture even further. You may or may not want to thin this out with more water.

 **6 to 10**

Ingredients:

- ▶ 1 pound green split peas
- ▶ 1 medium sweet potato, cut into 1-inch rounds
- ▶ 2 to 3 tablespoons Italian seasoning
- ▶ 1 teaspoon olive oil
- ▶ 1/2 teaspoon turmeric
- ▶ 1 teaspoon salt
- ▶ 1 teaspoon ground red chiles
- ▶ 1 tablespoon freshly ground black pepper
- ▶ 1 teaspoon cumin powder
- ▶ 8 cups water

Instructions:

Cook all ingredients in a crock pot until sweet potatoes are soft, about 6 hours. Transfer from the crock pot to a blender, and blend until smooth.

If you don't have a crock pot, put all the ingredients into a large roasting dish in the oven. Bake at 375° F until the vegetables are all cooked through. This can take anywhere from 2 to 3 hours. Make sure to cover the dish so the water does not evaporate.

Caldo Verde

Kale is a lovely vegetable. This soup will technically work with any hearty green, such as collard greens, mustard greens, or radish greens, but for some reason the kale just feels right. This is a staple dish in Portugal and is eaten with cornbread. Because it's got a mix of the potatoes and the leafy greens, you're eating something that will fill you up and still be a pleasure on the palate. If you are out of potatoes, chickpeas work just as well. Just make sure to cook the chickpeas beforehand or use canned. Beans like chickpeas take a long time to cook, and you'll be hungry long before dinner is served!

 ____ 4

Ingredients:

▶ 2 tablespoons olive oil

▶ 1 large onion, diced

▶ 3 cloves garlic, minced

▶ 1/4 teaspoon coarsely ground black pepper

▶ 2 pounds red potatoes (about 5 medium), halved

▶ 6 cups water

▶ 1 teaspoon salt

▶ 1 pound kale, finely sliced

Instructions:

Start with the olive oil in a large, deep pot. Heat the oil over high heat until a small wisp of smoke escapes the surface of the oil. Add in your onion, and a healthy pinch of salt. Stir the onions in the oil to coat the pieces, and then turn down the heat to medium. Allow the onions to slowly develop a brown color.

This should take 5 to 10 minutes, depending on how often you "check in" on them and stir them around. The longer you leave the onions alone, the easier it is for them to get properly browned.

Add the garlic to the browned onions, and stir through until just combined. Add your black pepper. Stir everything in the pot to combine it. Add the chopped potatoes, water, and salt. Put the lid on your pot, and turn up your heat to high. Let the water come to a full, rolling boil, and then reduce to a simmer, cover and let it simmer away for 30 to 45 minutes, or until the potatoes are soft. Using a potato masher or large wooden spoon, break up the potatoes as if to mash them. Leave enough chunks of potato (you don't want this to be smooth) but make sure to break up the large pieces. Add the kale to the potatoes in the pot and stir the ingredients to combine. Let the kale and potatoes simmer together for another 20 minutes, or until the kale is cooked to your liking. Taste for salt and adjust as needed.

Winter Melon Soup

Winter melon is a giant gourd-like thing grown traditionally in China but is also available in the United States. The texture, when cooked, is unmatched to anything else, and it's a mild, soothing experience to eat this vegetable.

10 to 12

Ingredients:

- ▶ 2 pounds winter melon, peeled of the outer skin and diced
- ▶ 1 pound potatoes, diced
- ▶ 1 pound carrots, diced
- ▶ 1 pound kale, roughly chopped
- ▶ 2 tablespoons whole fenugreek seeds
- ▶ 1 tablespoon chili powder
- ▶ 1 tablespoon salt
- ▶ 2 cans coconut milk

Instructions:

Dump the winter melon, potatoes, carrots, kale, fenugreek seeds, and chili powder into a large pot. Pour in just enough water to cover the vegetables. Bring the water to a full rolling boil, then reduce to a simmer.

With a spoon, take some of the cooking water and taste for salt. If it seems a little bland, this is OK, because a lot of the water will evaporate and concentrate the flavors. Cook 45 minutes. Taste the water again. If it's still not salty and spicy-hot enough for your liking, add more salt and chili powder until you have as much heat and salt as you like. Add coconut milk. Bring to a boil. Turn off the heat, and allow it to sit until you're ready to eat.

Note: This is perfect with a warm, crusty baguette. Simply wrap the baguette in a slightly damp towel, and bake in the oven at 350° F during the last 10 minutes of the soup's cooking. When the soup is ready, remove the baguette from the oven and take it out of the towel. Use oven mitts to do this, because the bread is hot. Slice the bread in half lengthwise and drizzle on a little olive oil. Sprinkle some salt and fresh parsley onto the halves of bread. Turn off the oven. Lay a dark-colored cloth napkin or kitchen towel in the bottom of a basket. Put the basket into the oven to warm. Cut the bread into 2-inch pieces. When you're done cutting, remove the basket from the oven and put the bread inside. Lay the edges of the towel over the bread. When you serve, lay the basket of bread next to the soup tureen and let each diner share the communal bread basket while eating the soup.

Fusion Sandwich

This is one of those that I'd take with me on those 4 and 5-hour road trips Mom and Dad loved to dash off on. Whenever we would go on vacation, it would be for long drives, instead of flying like sane people. To deal with the monotony of the road, my parents would encourage us to come up with interesting foods to take on the road. This sandwich is a modified version of the salad. Fortunately, because of its portability, it makes the perfect travel food. Unfortunately, if you're showing up to a large family gathering, there is bound to be food, and you'll be too sated to bother eating! Make this at your own risk, but know that you've been warned.

 4 to 6

Ingredients:

- ▶ 1 clove garlic, finely minced
- ▶ 1 tablespoon red wine vinegar
- ▶ 1 teaspoon salt
- ▶ 1 clove garlic, sliced in half lengthwise
- ▶ 1 eggplant, sliced into long planks, 1/2 inch thick
- ▶ 1 zucchini, sliced into long planks, 1/2 inch thick
- ▶ 1 portabella mushroom, sliced into strips, 1/2 inch thick
- ▶ 2 tablespoons olive oil
- ▶ 3 drops white truffle oil
- ▶ 1 tablespoon chopped thyme
- ▶ 1 tablespoon chopped oregano
- ▶ 1 tablespoon chopped basil
- ▶ 1 large baguette

Why roast?

The vegetables in this dish are fairly benign. They have their own flavors, but it's too subtle to come out in a sandwich, where you have other things in it. Roasting gives the vegetables an unmatched smoky flavor that you won't get with steaming or boiling. It is a relatively low-fat cooking technique and a nice way to get your needed servings of vegetables for the day.

Instructions:

In a bowl, combine the vinegar, garlic, and salt. Allow it to sit for the duration of your preparation. Rub the sliced garlic clove all over the baguette. This imparts a subtle garlic flavor that will permeate the bread.

Slice your vegetables into long planks or strips, as needed. To make it easier on yourself, use a serrated knife on the zucchini and the eggplant, because it will grip the vegetables better than a smooth-edged knife.

When all your vegetables are sliced, toss them in the olive oil and herbs, and lay them onto a wire rack. Place the wire rack over a baking sheet and bake in the oven, at 350° F for 20 to 25 minutes, or until they're golden brown. Check on your vegetables 10 minutes after heating initially, then every 5 minutes after that. Depending on your oven and how thick you cut the vegetables, you may need to adjust the cooking time.

In the last 5 minutes of roasting the vegetables, rub some water onto your bread and wrap it in foil. Place the loaf of bread on the second rack of your oven.

When the vegetables (and bread) are done, remove them from the oven. The bread will be especially hot, so handle with care. With a bread knife, cut the baguette loaf 3/4 of the way down, so as to leave a "hinge" on the loaf, and neatly stack your vegetables into the pocket you've formed. Drizzle the garlic/vinegar mixture and truffle oil over the vegetables. Close your "pocket" and wrap it up tightly with either a kitchen towel or plastic wrap. Place a large board over the loaf. Then, get some weights on top of the board. I use a few large cans of beans. In about 1 hour or so, your traveling sandwich will be ready to eat.

Dino Salad

This is a salad of the sort that I used to take with me for my lunch at school because it's really filling. I have expanded this to serve at parties, because it makes a beautiful, dramatic presentation on the table. You can either make this a layered salad (stack the layers from the bottom up), or toss everything through until well mixed. Both make for interesting presentations. I personally prefer to chop up the lettuces and all vegetables to the size of my mouth, so that there are no...awkward moments with errant dressing or people struggling with it. To make it easy on you, I've listed the ingredients in the order that I stack them. It's best to stack them on a very large platter, but if serving tossed, it looks best in a large salad bowl. I've included a dressing because it's complementary to the salad.

6

Ingredients:

▶ 1/2 pound romaine lettuce

▶ 1/4 pound mixed field greens

▶ 1/4 pound watercress

▶ 1 pound chickpeas

▶ 1/4 cup minced cilantro

▶ 1/4 cup minced flat-leaf parsley

▶ 1/2 pound Roma or plum tomatoes, cut into quarters lengthwise and sliced

▶ 1 large English cucumber, sliced in half lengthwise and thinly sliced

▶ 2 hass avocados, thinly sliced and arranged around the edges (or placed onto each serving if the salad is tossed)

▶ 1/4 pound chopped olives

Dressing

▶ 1 cup lemon juice

▶ 1 tablespoon tahini

▶ 2 tablespoons olive oil

▶ 1 tablespoon red pepper flakes (optional)

▶ 1 teaspoon salt, or more if desired

▶ 1 teaspoon freshly ground pepper

Instructions:

For the dressing: **Combine all ingredients in a blender or food processor on high.**

Lentils, Chickpeas, and Cashews

In July 2006, I went up to Ithaca, New York, to hang out with a large group of my vegan friends. We went to Buttermilk State Park and were having a potluck. Since most of us would be traveling in from various corners of North America, we were expecting mostly simple food without too many frills. I decided to knock everyone's socks off and serve them something that they would remember me by.

I was at Rich Bebenroth's house, where I invaded his kitchen. In addition to making a vat of soup the night before, I whipped some puri and roti, along with this dish to take to Ithaca. The lentils were the only thing to survive. It was a series of accidents!

Too wet!

Sometimes, when cooking, it's easy to get a particular dish too wet. To correct for this, you may want to add more cooked beans, rice, potatoes, or nuts to fill out the recipe. This is what happened in this recipe. When I was cooking, the dish came out way too wet for my liking, because the can of tomato was too large for the amount of chickpeas I had in the dish. I added the lentils to round it out.

Originally, I was supposed to just be making a daal-like thing with the chickpeas. Unfortunately, the can of chickpeas was far outstripped by the tomatoes. In a panic, I flew around Rich's small New York kitchen, and searched for something, anything to get me out of this bind. In went the rest of the lentils he had. Then, by the time the lentils were cooked, it was missing something, so in went the cashews and lemon juice. Rich had a whole bunch of thyme, so that went in as well.

By the time we got the food to upstate New York (while contentedly munching away at the flatbreads on the way there), I was horrified that it would be a giant flop at the potluck. There I was, chatting away with my friends. They wanted to know what to do with the lentils thing, so I advised that they just use it like a dip for tortilla chips. I got back on the cool grass and continued chattering on. I got up to take a look in the box to see if I could snag a bit of it.

Oops. It was finished in the space of 15 minutes. People were eating it straight up, over hummus, with tortilla chips, and pretty much every other manner you could imagine a thick salsa-like chickpeas-and-beans dish to be eaten. The interesting thing is that although it didn't taste like anything anyone had ever had before, I found my friends experimenting with the dish, trying it in different ways right there at the picnic.

After testing this recipe, my friends found that you have a lot of wiggle room with the beans, tomatoes, and water. The other neat thing is that this is one of those "wing it" dishes. If you don't have vodka, use red wine, or leave it out all together.

If you do somehow end up with leftovers (if you didn't take it to a potluck and watch it disappear before your eyes), it will definitely taste better the next day. Use it between two slices of bread as a sandwich. Try it thinned out a bit with some water, and served with rice. Try it tossed with pasta. Take it straight up and watch your coworkers drool as the lovely smells fill the room when you heat up your lunch in the microwave. Freeze the leftovers! They keep rather well.

If you're out of cilantro, use basil. If you can't for the life of you find where you put those bay leaves, it'll be fine without them. The spices and nuts are the key to this dish turning out a success. It's that subtle interplay between the different spices, the tomato, beans, and nuts that gives this dish its signature kick. If you can't find cashews, then peanuts or pistachios would be just fine.

Ingredients:

- ▶ 3 tablespoons oil
- ▶ 1 teaspoon mustard seeds
- ▶ 1 teaspoon cumin seeds
- ▶ 1 large onion, finely minced
- ▶ 2 cloves garlic
- ▶ 2 medium carrots, chopped
- ▶ 1/2 teaspoon turmeric
- ▶ Salt
- ▶ 1/2 teaspoon clove powder
- ▶ 1/2 teaspoon cinnamon
- ▶ 1/8 teaspoon nutmeg
- ▶ 1 tablespoon thyme
- ▶ 2 dried bay leaves (or 3 fresh)
- ▶ 1 whole dried chile
- ▶ 3 cups chopped tomato
- ▶ 1 cup vodka
- ▶ 8 ounces uncooked lentils
- ▶ 8 ounces cooked chickpeas (1 can)
- ▶ 6 cups water
- ▶ 1 cup raw cashews
- ▶ 1 lemon, juiced
- ▶ 1/4 cup chopped cilantro (optional)
- ▶ Freshly ground black pepper

Instructions:

In a wok or large pot, pour in the oil and wait for it to heat up over high heat. When it gets hot enough that a small wisp of smoke escapes the surface, add the mustard seeds. Wait about 30 seconds, or until they pop. Add the cumin seeds. Wait for the cumin to pop and subside. This should take only a few seconds.

Add the onions, garlic, carrots, turmeric, salt to taste, clove, cinnamon, nutmeg, thyme, dried chile, and bay leaves. Stir the ingredients in the pot to combine everything. When the onions are all turned evenly yellow (from the turmeric), things are properly combined. Turn down the heat to medium and begin dicing the tomatoes. If the tomatoes are canned, drain off the liquid and reserve it.

After about 5 minutes, the onions should be softened. Pour in the tomatoes and vodka. Stir everything around in the pot to combine the ingredients thoroughly. When the liquid comes to a full boil, pour in the reserved tomato liquid if using canned. Wait 5 minutes, or until the mixture of tomatoes and spices is thicker.

Add the cooked chickpeas, uncooked lentils, and about 3 cups of the water. Add the cashews and cover the pot. Increase the heat to high and let it come to a full, rolling boil. Leave the water boiling until the lentils are cooked through, adding more water as the pot dries out. This should take 30 minutes.

Finish the dish with the lemon juice, cilantro, and black pepper to taste. Continue boiling, until it reaches the consistency of a thick salsa.

Chapter 2:
Back to the Basics

These recipes are generally simple to make, and involve making things in their most stripped-down manner. I would use these as a primer for beginner vegan cooks to get them started in their adventures. These are the sorts of things one serves when trying to avoid damaged egos from being unable to handle actual flavor. It's the sort of thing I'd call "mixed-company" food. If you don't know what the rules are to begin with, how can you break them with any level of confidence? That's what I'd like for this to be—your baseline from which you can deviate as much as you want, once you master the techniques.

As with most rules, you'll certainly find your own way of doing things that works for you. My mother was never a fan of the oven, and she would avoid it like the plague. Instead of making leavened breads, she would make flatbreads, delicious and steamy direct from the stovetop. Instead of casseroles, she would make these complex stews and soups from a variety of vegetables, then serve them over piping-hot rice to give that satisfaction.

That's what I'm hoping this section does for you. I want you to get your feet wet, and then see how you can make it work for your own comfort level. Not comfortable with the stovetop? Use an oven or microwave! Don't like using the large oven? The toaster oven is the ideal tool for any person pressed for space or wanting to avoid using so much gas or electricity.

Improvise as needed whenever you can.

Dry-Cooked Chickpeas

I love this either mashed up and spread onto my bread when I make sandwiches, or served with some good basmati rice. It's also excellent with any Indian flatbreads. It's a large-ish quantity, because there's really no sense in using that many different spices, and have a tiny little dish of food to show for it. Ground spices will not work in lieu of the whole ones in this particular recipe. I'm using cooked chickpeas for this, so you may substitute canned. This dish works well in nonstick cookware, so if you have it, use it.

 6

Ingredients:

- ▶ 2 pounds cooked chickpeas (canned is ideal—just drain the water).

Whole spices

- ▶ 1 teaspoon cumin seeds
- ▶ 1 teaspoon black mustard seeds
- ▶ 2 teaspoons coriander seeds, crushed (place in a zip-lock bag and crush with a rolling pin)

Ground spices

- ▶ 1 teaspoon turmeric
- ▶ 1 teaspoon chili powder
- ▶ Salt and freshly ground black pepper

Aromatics

- ▶ 5 cloves of garlic, minced
- ▶ 1 large onion, chopped fine
- ▶ 2 stalks curry leaves, if available
- ▶ Fresh herbs
- ▶ 1/4 cup minced cilantro, for garnish

Oils

- ▶ 2 tablespoons peanut, canola, or safflower oil
- ▶ 2 tablespoons sesame oil

Instructions:

Heat both oils in a wok or large, shallow pan on high heat. Add the whole spices. When the spices begin to pop, wait 10 more seconds and add all of the aromatics. Sauté until the onions are soft. Add the ground turmeric and 1 teaspoon salt and stir through. Cook for another minute. Add the beans. Toss gently until all the beans are yellow. Cook for 5 more minutes.

Add chili powder. Toss through until thoroughly combined.

At this point, taste a bean or two. If it needs more heat, add some ground black pepper. If it needs more salt, sprinkle on some more salt, and cook for an additional 5 minutes. Remove from the heat, and sprinkle on the chopped cilantro over the top as garnish. You may use more or less as your tastes dictate. This will also work with Italian flat-leaf parsley instead of cilantro.

Generic Accompaniment
to Dry-Cooked Anything

Ingredients:

▶ 1 large English cucumber

▶ 5 Thai bird chiles

▶ 1 small onion

▶ Lemon juice

▶ Salt

Why dry roast?

Soups, stews, and sauces are all well and good. However, there are times when you want a dish to be dry-cooked, to be able to incorporate it into different applications. This is what I did with the Dry-Cooked Chickpeas (page 52). I wanted to get a recipe that I could easily use with bread, rice, or salad, without making everything a huge mess. The dry-cooking technique is good for any bean you can drain and wash off. The accompaniment I have provided here works just as well with dry-roasted potatoes.

Instructions:

Dice the cucumber and sprinkle lightly with salt. Set aside to drain. Finely dice the onions and mince the chiles. Marinate the onions and chiles in the lemon juice. Strain out the cucumber after 1/2 hour of "soaking" in the sprinkling of salt. Toss to combine.

You may omit the chiles or reduce the amount, but having that kick along with the cooling, refreshing cucumber is a really nice contrast.

Unslaw

I was thinking of foods that made people cringe, and cabbage came to mind. People usually associate it with a stinky smell and don't know how to make it correctly. This Christmas, try my cabbage "salad" for a red and green combo that's sure to please.

> **What are caraway seeds?**
>
> Caraway seeds, like their friends the cumin seeds, are perfect with any sort of cabbage-like vegetable. This particular seasoning mix would work equally well with cauliflower, bok choy, or red cabbage. Make sure to adjust cooking times. The seeds bring out the natural flavor of the cabbage without the bad smell ordinarily associated with cabbage and other vegetables like it. Trust me, you'll love it.

That said, another disgusting innovation of nonvegans is coleslaw. Never have I seen a more disgusting way to treat a vegetable. Who in their right mind would think that eggs, salt, oil, fat, and raw cabbage would taste good? Oh, and you have to serve it alongside something dripping with even more grease, because that's the American Way.

And sauerkraut? Are you kidding me? You take a bunch of salt, smother the cabbage with it, and let it ferment. At the end of a few weeks, you have this vile-smelling rot that people actually relish (haha, pun) eating over some dead thing. It's grotesque.

Cabbage deserves far better press than it's been getting. I'm its chief PR guy, and I'm going to make sure that nobody maligns this poor vegetable in my presence again! Power to the cabbage!

 6

Ingredients:

- ▶ 1/4 head red cabbage
- ▶ 1/4 head green cabbage
- ▶ 1 leek
- ▶ 1 tablespoon vegetable oil
- ▶ 1 teaspoon caraway seeds
- ▶ 1 teaspoon cumin
- ▶ 1 teaspoon black mustard seeds
- ▶ 1 teaspoon turmeric
- ▶ 1 carrot, grated
- ▶ Salt
- ▶ Chili powder

Instructions:

Cut the cabbage in half lengthwise. Remove the core with a paring knife. Slice it into threads by making horizontal cuts across the head. Do the same for the leek and the green cabbage. Heat the oil. Add the mustard seeds. When it starts to pop (up to 1 minute), add the caraway and cumin seeds. When both begin to pop, add the leeks and carrots. Sprinkle in some salt and turmeric. Sauté until the vegetables soften, stirring constantly.

Add the green and red cabbage. Lightly sprinkle with salt. Toss vigorously in the pan, until all the vegetable matter is coated evenly with spice and oil. At this point, check for salt and heat. If it tastes too mild for your liking, add some chili powder. Allow the chili powder or salt to cook in for a minute before tasting again.

Warning: Do not allow the cabbage to cook for more than 10 minutes. You want to retain the colors and texture. It's supposed to be just cooked. You should be able to feel the crunch.

Remove from heat after 5 minutes and serve as a side dish to a hearty meal, such as those slow cooker recipes.

Variation:

After the cabbage is done, add 3 or 4 tablespoons of tahini and mix it through.

Brutus Salad

Just as Brutus killed Caesar, so shall this salad destroy that limp, watery mass called a Caesar salad (which I generally couldn't eat, because Caesar dressings typically contain eggs and anchovy). Once, at a company's annual banquet, they asked if I would like a vegetarian meal. The vegetarian meal (not salad, but the rest of the food) turned out to be a vegan meal, but that's beside the point. The point is that they managed to screw up a basic green salad. They served Caesar salad. Unfortunately, back in those days I was a lacto-ovo vegetarian, so I ate the limp, squalid greens swimming in their eggy dressing. It was so disgusting that I couldn't take another bite without wanting to emit the contents of my stomach all over the jerk who was saying, "In France, we would have some real meat, like beef, to start the meal. This is so cheap." I seriously wanted to do very not vegan things to his face at that point, but civility prevailed. By the time I got home, I was so livid at the whole farce that they called a banquet that I immediately invented this dish on the spot. I figured that I could definitely do better in my sleep than the inept cooks at the hall. Apparently, I was right.

 4 to 6

Ingredients:

- ▶ 1 head romaine lettuce
- ▶ 1/2 pound watercress
- ▶ 1 teaspoon lemon juice
- ▶ 1 tablespoon orange reduction (orange juice reduced to 1/4 the original volume on low heat, or just use frozen orange juice concentrate)
- ▶ Salt and freshly ground black pepper
- ▶ 3 tablespoons olive oil.

Instructions:

Chop lettuce into bite-size pieces. Dump on the washed watercress. Pitch the mix into a bowl.

Combine the lemon juice, orange juice, and salt and whisk until dissolved. Add black pepper and combine. Add olive oil. Whisk vigorously to make a dressing.

Mixed Greens Composed Salad

My friend Jenna in New Jersey was getting married. What should have been a happy occasion was quickly turning ugly, because her omnivorous family and caterers were giving her grief over her desire for a vegan menu. Fortunately for the cows, chickens, and fish, Jenna knew that what should be a celebration of life should have nothing associated with death in it. Instead of caving in to pressure from others, Jenna stuck to her guns.

However, they did have a point. Caterers can be rather clueless when it comes to serving vegans. Rather than take a chance of the caterers serving tofu burgers and soy hot dogs because that's what they think we're capable of eating, Jenna asked me for help. I compiled a menu that would be easy for the caterers to prepare and that involved ingredients they could get hold of easily. I didn't include any of the fake meats, because that's not how I work.

I figured that this would be an excellent addition to the basics section, because it is so simple to put together but looks so fancy on the plate. It would be a filling starter to a formal dinner that you're hosting. It would also be a great way to make your coworkers or schoolmates jealous. They'll be eating air bread (bread that's mostly air, not actual bread) and some dead thing. You'll be having what looks like nature's bounty exploding onto your plate.

If you have any nice greens that you like eating raw, feel free to add those as well. This is the time to experiment and see what you like. The dressing, while not integral to the dish, is a good starter dressing for anyone who isn't familiar with making salad dressings that involve strictly vegan ingredients. The creamy sesame seeds and tahini don't weigh the salad down—instead, they enhance the fresh green textures in the leaves.

As with any composed salad, you want the vegetables cut into pieces just big enough to fit onto the end of your fork. It looks really gross to see little bits of vegetables dangling out of people's mouths as they eat, and having to cut up salad at the table takes far more effort for the diner. Be considerate to the people you're serving, and they will thank you by coming back for more and more!

Because of the amount of nuts in this salad, you don't really need croutons. If you absolutely must have croutons, feel free to use your favorite recipe or the one in this book (page 119). Additionally, this would be a good place to add things like falafel, toast points, potato patties (page 63), or any other crispy sort of thing you like. I have had good results with stacking bajji (page 90) or pakora (page 96) on top of my salad. There is something about fried foods on salad that seems so sinful, yet so tasty!

 12

Ingredients:

- 1 pound romaine lettuce
- 1 pound mixed field greens
- 1/2 pound watercress
- 2 pound chickpeas
- 1/2 pound chopped olives
- 1 pound Roma or plum tomatoes, cut into quarters lengthwise and sliced
- 1 pound large English cucumber, cut in half lengthwise and thinly sliced
- 2 hass avocados, thinly sliced and

arranged around edges (or placed onto each serving if salad is tossed)

- Sprinkling of lemon juice.
- 1/4 cup minced cilantro
- 1/4 cup minced flat-leaf parsley
- 1/4 cup walnut halves
- 1/4 cup pecan halves
- 1/4 cup cashew halves

Dressing

- 1 cup lemon juice
- 1 cup sesame seeds
- 1 tablespoon tahini

- 1/4 cup cashews
- 2 tablespoons olive oil
- 1 tablespoon red pepper flakes (optional)
- 1 teaspoon salt, or more if desired
- 1 teaspoon freshly ground pepper

Instructions:

Stack the vegetables in layers and sprinkle the herbs, nuts, and lemon juice on top. Combine all dressing ingredients in a blender or food processor on high until smooth. Serve dressing on the side. Scale the recipe up or down as needed.

Palm Hearts

Palm hearts are good cold, but grilling them gives a beautiful contrast in color. The insides will be blindingly white, while the outsides will be mildly darker. This salad, with its bursts of cooling freshness, will provide considerable workouts for those who like to sink their teeth into their dinners. However, if you cannot grill them, just use them plain, and the dish will still be delicious.

 4 to 6

Ingredients:

- 1 pound palm hearts, grilled lightly and diced
- 1/4 pound tomatoes, diced
- 1 small carrot, grated
- 1/2 medium onion, diced
- 1/4 cup frozen grated coconut
- 1/4 cup lemon juice
- Salt and freshly ground black pepper
- 1/4 cup minced cilantro, for garnish

Instructions:

Awaken the coconut from its frozen state by heating it over low heat on the stove. Some fat will render out of the coconut, but if you're nervous about the pan being that dry, you can throw some water in. You just want to smell the coconut, and it'll be done.

Combine all the ingredients (except salt), and toss with the lemon. Chill in the fridge until cold. Add salt and pepper to taste. Scatter on the cilantro leaves for a garnish. You may use more or less as your taste decrees.

Basic Spiced Broccoli

I was at some function or another for work that had a really bad menu for vegans. It consisted of limp, dead-looking romaine lettuce smothered in Caesar dressing, some steamed broccoli, and pasta with steamed vegetables. I got really annoyed that something as tasty as broccoli could be messed up to that level. Instead of stewing in my juices, I came home and whipped up a couple of easy recipes. This is what I came up with for a basic broccoli.

 4 to 6

Ingredients:

- ▶ 2 tablespoons oil
- ▶ Zest of one lime
- ▶ Juice of one lime
- ▶ 1/2 teaspoon chili powder
- ▶ 1 teaspoon garlic powder
- ▶ 1 teaspoon cumin powder
- ▶ 1 tablespoon sesame seeds (optional)
- ▶ Salt
- ▶ 1 head broccoli, cut into florets

Instructions:

Preheat the oven to 350° F. In a bowl, combine the oil, lime zest, lime juice, chili powder, garlic powder, cumin powder, sesame seeds, and salt. Blend to make a loose paste. Toss broccoli florets in the oil, lime, and spice mixture. Bake in the oven, covered, at 350° F for 30 minutes. Remove the cover, sprinkle on the sesame seeds, and bake for 5 more minutes, uncovered. This is a perfect side dish, but it also does really well when added to creamy pasta dishes.

Basic Spiced Cauliflower

Sometimes, you just want to have the simple flavors of the vegetable by itself without a lot of complex ones getting in the way. I like this when I'm having warm flatbread. This was the second recipe in that series of basics that I came up with.

It's funny, though. I don't think that once it's cooked, cauliflower has much of a taste in general. With this particular vegetable, I find that I'm looking for the texture more than anything else. Be careful not to overcook your cauliflower, or you'll end up with a disgusting mash that is decidedly unpleasant.

Another neat thing about this recipe is that since cauliflower is so neutral in flavor, it absorbs the spices and tastes even better the next day.

4 to 6

Ingredients:

- ▶ 1 head cauliflower, cut into florets
- ▶ 2 tablespoons oil
- ▶ 1/2 teaspoon curry power
- ▶ Salt

Instructions:

Toss cauliflower in the oil and curry powder. Sprinkle with salt. Cook at 400° F in the oven for 15 minutes. Serve with flatbread.

Fast Cauliflower

I can't really call this a proper aloo gobi, an Indian potato and cauliflower dish that involves a long list of spices, multiple cooking techniques, and an iron will, as it is prone to burning and other disasters. This is my college-dormitory answer to the "proper" Indian version. Try this in warmed pita bread, over rice, or as a simple side dish.

🕰 **4 to 6**

Ingredients:

- ▶ 1 teaspoon cumin powder
- ▶ 1 teaspoon coriander seeds, crushed
- ▶ 1 teaspoon sesame seeds
- ▶ 2 teaspoons oil
- ▶ 1/2 teaspoon salt
- ▶ 1/2 teaspoon freshly ground black pepper
- ▶ 1/4 teaspoon turmeric
- ▶ 1/4 cup water
- ▶ 1 head cauliflower
- ▶ 2 medium potatoes

Instructions:

Combine the cumin powder, coriander seeds, sesame seeds, oil, salt, pepper, turmeric, and water in a blender, and pulse until all the ingredients are combined. If you don't have a blender, just mixing it together with a fork or whisk will do just fine. Separate the cauliflower into medium-sized florets, and cube the potatoes into 1/2-inch cubes.

Toss the cauliflower, potatoes, and spice mixture together until combined. Microwave on high for 8 to 10 minutes, or until the potatoes and cauliflower are cooked through. If you don't have a microwave, you can bake this at 350° F for 30 to 45 minutes.

Basic Mushrooms

These are basic sautéed mushrooms. You can serve them as a side dish or add them to other recipes.

 4

Ingredients:

- ▶ 3 tablespoons olive oil
- ▶ 4 large portabella mushrooms (stems too, please), thinly sliced
- ▶ Salt
- ▶ 1 teaspoon Italian seasoning
- ▶ 1 clove of garlic, crushed and minced
- ▶ 1/4 cup minced flat-leaf parsley

Instructions:

Heat oil in a wide, shallow pan. Get it very hot. Add the mushrooms, and sprinkle on salt to taste. Allow them to cook for about 10 seconds before disturbing—you want them to sear. Toss around in the pan. Add Italian seasoning. Add garlic. Stir for about 10 minutes, to allow it to get less watery. Remove from heat and stir in the parsley.

Demonic Mushrooms

This demonic stuff has the kick of a horse. I do not take responsibility for anyone who suffers third-degree burns from eating this dish. People who have made this dish during testing have said that it becomes disturbingly addictive. I have seen this in person: you start with eating just one or two, and suddenly you realize that you have just snuck a few more and don't have any left.

 4

Ingredients:

- ▶ 1 pound white button mushrooms, stems set aside
- ▶ 3 tablespoons canola oil
- ▶ 3 ounces jalapeño peppers
- ▶ 3 tablespoons olive oil
- ▶ 1 teaspoon chili powder
- ▶ White truffle oil (optional)
- ▶ 8 ounces black olives
- ▶ 1 tablespoon minced thyme

Instructions:

Remove stems from the mushrooms. Toss the caps with canola oil. Slice the jalapeño peppers as thinly as you can. Depending on your own taste, lay 1 to 3 slices on top of your mushrooms. In a food processor, combine the mushroom stems, olive oil, chili powder, truffle oil, and olives, and pulse until the olives and mushrooms are diced. Lay the mixture into the mushroom caps. Sprinkle on thyme. Bake in a 350° F oven for 15 minutes.

Basic Potatoes

With small red or new potatoes, you want to have the mildly sweet, delicate flavor and texture of the potatoes all by themselves. This dish showcases the potatoes beautifully and allows you to enjoy them fully.

 6

Ingredients:

- 5 pounds small red potatoes
- Salt
- 3 tablespoons olive oil
- Minced parsley

Instructions:

Add the potatoes to a pot and fill with cold water. Bring the water to a full boil, and liberally salt the water until it is salty like the sea. Reduce heat to a simmer, and simmer for 10 to 12 minutes. Remove from heat and drain off the water. Toss with oil and sprinkle salt on top. Put in a 500° F oven for up to 10 minutes to develop crispy skin. Remove from heat. Toss with parsley.

Asian Roasted Potatoes

As you can probably tell, I really enjoy potatoes in every form that I can find. This is another one of those simple potato recipes that looks pretty on the plate and tastes interestingly good.

 6

Ingredients:

- 5 pounds red new potatoes
- 2 tablespoons sesame seeds
- 2 tablespoons sesame oil
- 3 tablespoons rice wine vinegar
- Salt and cracked black pepper

Instructions:

Toss all ingredients together, coating the taters evenly. Spread out on a baking sheet in a single layer. Bake at 350° F for 20 minutes, then at 500° F for another 5 minutes. Toss the potatoes gently with the vinegar. Serve as an accompaniment to a light stir-fry meal.

Baked Potato Rounds

For the "potatoes and potatoes" vegan in your life. While baked potatoes taste really good, they're a mess to eat, and often require margarine or other unsavory ingredients. These can be eaten in one or two bites. Choose potatoes that are long and slender to avoid having people get messy. You may vary this with Yukon Gold or fingerling potatoes for a different texture, but make sure to adjust your cooking times, because these tender potatoes cook more quickly. There's no need to peel the potatoes as long as you clean them thoroughly.

I talked about this recipe with a friend of mine, who is the mother of a four-year-old. She told me that ever since she read it, she made it multiple times because it was an easy snack that was not too complicated for her child to eat, and it avoided making a giant mess in the kitchen or paying a small fortune for something processed to within an inch of its life. Because they are easy to pick up, these rounds work beautifully for children still exploring food.

 1 to 4

Ingredients:

- ▶ 1 Idaho baking potato, cut into 1/2-inch disks
- ▶ 2 tablespoons olive oil
- ▶ 1 teaspoon paprika
- ▶ Salt and freshly ground black pepper
- ▶ Chopped chives (reserve)

Instructions:

In a large zip-top bag, combine potato rounds, olive oil, paprika, and salt and pepper to taste. Close the top and make sure it's sealed. Shake the bag around and rub the potato rounds through the bag to make sure they get well coated. If you don't have a zip-top bag, you may coat the potatoes with a pastry brush and evenly sprinkle on the spices.

Lay them onto a baking sheet in a single layer. Bake at 350° F about 20 minutes, or until tender. Sprinkle on chives.

Variations:

You really don't want to combine these variations. These are to be mixed with the potatoes before baking. Instead of just salt and pepper, here are some other spices that go well with potatoes:

- ▶ 1 tablespoon curry powder
- ▶ 1 teaspoon each of cumin, black mustard, and coriander seeds, ground
- ▶ 1/4 cup of finely minced parsley
- ▶ 1 tablespoon minced thyme
- ▶ Sprinkling of cayenne pepper
- ▶ Broccoli florets on top, with an extra drizzle of olive oil and sprinkle of salt.

Herb-Crusted Potato Patties

This was one of those recipes that began its life as a colossal disaster. For whatever reason, it was a disappointment to my testers, who had been used to getting all sorts of recipes that were really spot-on for them. After serious tweaking and retesting, it became a solid recipe with a taste that people do like.

 4 to 6

Ingredients:

- ▶ 3 pounds potatoes, baked and gently mashed (1/2 bakers and 1/2 red)
- ▶ 1 tablespoon salt
- ▶ 3 tablespoon dried basil
- ▶ 3 tablespoon dried thyme
- ▶ 1 tablespoon freshly ground black pepper
- ▶ Roughly 1 cup breadcrumbs
- ▶ Oil for shallow frying (about 2 inches deep)

Sauce

- ▶ 1/4 cup oil
- ▶ 1 tomato, finely diced
- ▶ Up to 1 teaspoon salt
- ▶ 2 tablespoons red chile flakes
- ▶ 1 clove garlic

Instructions:

Bake and gently smash the potatoes (you want some lumps in there). In a food processor combine the spices, and then toss through the breadcrumbs. Combine with the potatoes. You want a mixture that's on the dry side, and will hold together in a ball. You may need to add more breadcrumbs as needed to make the balls take shape and form tight patties. Make the potatoes into balls about 1/4 cup in size.

Set aside, and cool in the fridge for one hour. Remove from fridge and gently press down the center of the potato ball to make a flat patty. Fry in the heated oil for 2 to 4 minutes per side, until browned. Drain on a wire rack.

Make the sauce as soon as the potatoes come out of the fridge. Heat the oil in a pan, and add the tomato and the salt. Let it cook down for about 5 minutes. Reduce the heat to as low as it will go and gently simmer until all the potatoes are done.

When ready to serve, add the chile flakes and garlic to the hot tomato mixture, and blend in a food processor or blender until smooth.

Beeten Potatoes

I strongly dislike beets. This is more or less the only way I'll eat them, because they have a smoother taste and texture than canned beets. The potatoes and dill just round out the flavor enough that you can take advantage of the pretty color of the beets without having too much of their taste powering through the dish. I do like this over a salad, because the colors and textures look so nice on a white plate.

If you're a beet lover to the max, feel free to add a few more beets. Don't worry about it too much, because you've got a lot of potatoes to beet up!

 **4 to 6**

Ingredients:

- 3 medium-sized beets, cut into 1/4-inch slices
- 15 small red potatoes
- 375 ml red or white wine (half a bottle)
- 1/2 teaspoon allspice
- 1/4 cup red wine vinegar
- 1/2 cup water
- 1/4 cup raspberry preserves
- 3 tablespoons sugar
- 2 to 5 tablespoons olive oil
- Large handful of fresh dill
- 3 tablespoons grated ginger
- Salt

Instructions:

Fill a large stockpot 3/4 of the way with cold water. Add the potatoes to the pot, and place on a stove over high heat. In a skillet, pour in the wine, the red wine vinegar, the raspberry preserves, and the water. Increase the heat to medium-high. If you don't have the raspberry preserves, you may use apple jam, strawberry jam, or marmalade. If you don't have any of those, feel free to use pineapple juice instead.

Both these liquids should take anywhere from 10 to 15 minutes to come up to heat. While they're going, remove the stem and root from the beets, and slice them about 1/4 inch thick. Don't bother peeling them because they will stain everything and make a mess. It's not worth it.

When your beets are all sliced up, slide them into the skillet that has the wine, vinegar, and water. Don't worry if the liquids haven't boiled yet. Sprinkle in the sugar over the beets. Grab two large pinches of salt and sprinkle over the beets.

Start chopping the dill as fine as you can get it. When the dill is chopped, grate the ginger.

By now, the water should be boiling, and the wine should be bubbling. Turn down both burners on the stove to medium-low. You want them to simmer, not boil. Boiling makes the beets bitter and makes the potatoes fall apart. If, by mistake, the pan gets too hot, and the liquid has been boiling for any length of time, add some additional sugar to round out the flavor.

Once the liquid in the pan with the beets and wine has come down to a gentle simmer, add the ginger and the allspice.

In a large bowl, combine the dill and olive oil. Have it waiting for when the beets and potatoes are finished cooking.

With a fork, poke one of the beets. If you feel no resistance, the beets are finished cooking. If you find that the beets are taking too long to cook, give them a quick spin in the microwave for 7 to 10 minutes to get them all the way tender.

Remove the beets from the skillet, and add the beets along with the liquids to the bowl with the dill and oil in it. Toss gently to combine the beets with the oil and herbs.

Place the skillet back on the stove and increase the heat to high. Whisk vigorously until the liquid gets thick and syrupy. When it's at the desired consistency, remove the skillet from the heat, and pour it over the beets. Toss the beets and liquid to combine.

With a fork, poke one of the red potatoes. If you feel no resistance, the potatoes are done. Drain them in a colander, liberally sprinkle with salt, and toss to combine. Add the potatoes to the bowl with the beets. Gently toss the ingredients to combine.

You might serve this as one in a series of appetizers. This dish also works well in a salad. If you take some out, mash zit, and stuff it into a pita bread, all you'd need is some lettuce and tomato to make a smashing sandwich. Toss with some cooked brown rice for a nice, comforting side dish. Chill it and serve cold for a lovely potato salad. Experiment with other juices, wines, and liquors to find a combination that works for you.

Jimmy Crack Corn Crack

These are godly good. These are so good that I know for a fact that we ate roughly 4 apiece while I was making them. We were supposed to have wound up with around 4 dozen. I think maybe 2 dozen actually survived to get to the table. And then at the table we ate more. This stuff is like crack but in corn form. They're delicious in the plain version, but we noticed astronomical flavor from just a few simple spices.

 6 to 10

Ingredients:

- ▶ 3 (12-ounce) cans sweet corn, drained
- ▶ 4 cups finely ground yellow cornmeal
- ▶ 1/4 onion, diced or grated
- ▶ About 3 cans' worth of water (using a corn can to measure) worth of water
- ▶ Salt
- ▶ Spices to taste (optional, see variations below)

Instructions:

Preheat your cast iron skillet over medium-low heat. If you're using a nonstick skillet, heat it over a medium heat. You want it hot enough to be able to heat the corn for an extended browning time without burning it.

What is cornmeal?

There is a difference between corn flour (also known as Maseca in some Latin American stores), cornmeal, and cornstarch. Please do not confuse them! Cornstarch is a very fine white powder used to thicken sauces and make glazes. Corn flour is used in dishes like tamales, and is about the consistency of all-purpose flour. Cornmeal is ground corn, and has the texture of grits or farina (cream of wheat). All are versatile.

Mix the canned corn, salt, and cornmeal together in a large bowl (about double the volume of the three ingredients to avoid making a mess), tossing evenly with your hands. We didn't add any salt at all, because the corn was not fresh, and it still tasted wonderful.

Pour in your first can of water. Mix the water and cornmeal and corn mixture with your hands as much as you can. There will still be a lot of dry cornmeal in the bowl. This is a good thing. Add the onion and any additional spices and mix in to the best of your ability. Add the second can of water and stir through. You'll notice the batter feels fairly thick. You want the consistency to be about as thick as bread dough, only wetter.

Grab a small handful in your palm and roll around to make a ball. Press down gently to form a soft patty approximately 2 inches wide and 1 inch thick. If the round patties aren't sticking together, stir in some extra cornmeal until they form wet, soft patties.

Lay the patties flat onto the hot skillet. With a small teaspoon, drizzle a few drops of oil around the edges of the corn fritter. If the fritters are browning too quickly, or you smell a burning smell or see too much smoke, remove the pan from the stove to allow it to cool down, and decrease the heat.

About 1 minute after laying the corn fritters onto the hot skillet, the bottom side should be lightly browned. Flip the fritters over and drizzle on a few more drops around the edges. In another minute or two, the cake should be cooked on the other side. If you would like them to be a darker brown, cook them longer.

Drain on a wire rack. Leftovers may be frozen and reheated later in the toaster oven.

Variations:

1 tablespoon paprika, 1 tablespoon coriander powder, 1 tablespoon cumin powder, and 3 tablespoons coconut milk. Add an additional 3 tablespoons cornmeal to even out the added liquid.

Indian Roasted Potatoes

Back in India, the only people to own an oven were the bakers and those who were mind-bogglingly wealthy. This means that the Indian cook needs to improvise, and make this dish over the stovetop, constantly watching it and fearing that the whole mess won't form a crust and get properly cooked.

If you have the luxury of an oven, as most in America do, use it! This is my own variation on the classic dish, which uses russets, because I find that the contrasting textures of the potatoes and the other vegetables is really a change from anything you'd get elsewhere. It's a personal preference that you can do without if you don't want to bother with it. Just plain Idaho baking potatoes work perfectly.

These sorts of dishes are eaten as one of many accompaniments to one main bed of rice or bread, and many little cups of different varieties that each diner eats. But be careful—these things go as fast as homemade croutons!

A good point to mention: if this had been part of a typical Indian meal, you would have had a small bed of rice on your plate, surrounded by sambhar/rasam, some steamed vegetables, some fresh raw vegetables, some pickles, some small amount of stir-fried vegetables.

 10 to 12

Ingredients:

- 1 pound Yukon gold potatoes
- 1 pound red potatoes
- 1 pound white potatoes
- 1 pound russet potatoes
- 1 pound Idaho baking potatoes (dice all potatoes to about 2 inches square)
- 1/4 cup peanut, canola, or safflower oil
- 2 teaspoon cumin seeds
- 2 teaspoon black mustard seeds
- 1/2 teaspoon yellow split peas (this is to be used as a spice)
- Handful of curry leaves, if available
- 1 whole chile, sliced lengthwise
- 1 teaspoon salt
- 1 teaspoon turmeric
- 1 teaspoon ground coriander seed

Instructions:

In a roasting dish, heat the oil. Add the cumin seeds and mustard seeds. Wait until they crackle and pop like mad (about 1 minute). Add the split peas. Roast gently for 5 seconds. Tear the curry leaves in half and add them. Immediately add the potatoes and chile. Sprinkle on the salt, coriander, and turmeric. Toss through until the color is all yellow. Bake in an oven at 375° F until fork tender (usually 30 minutes in my oven).

Serve with rice, roti (page 112), or puri (page 113).

Lentils

I love lentil soup, but it doesn't allow me much in the way of doing stuff with it. I prefer to cook the lentils, drain them, and use them like regular beans. After that, I'll use them in soups and the like. What really irritates me, however, is how easy it is to find nonvegan lentil soup. It does not need bacon, people! Lentils are so creamy and delicious all on their own that you just need a few spices to brighten up their texture.

🕐 ____ **6**

Ingredients:

- ▶ 1 tablespoon peanut oil
- ▶ 1/2 teaspoon cumin seeds
- ▶ 1 tablespoon sesame seeds
- ▶ 1 large onion, chopped
- ▶ 2 cloves of garlic, crushed
- ▶ Handful curry leaves (optional)
- ▶ Pinch of asafetida
- ▶ 1 teaspoon turmeric
- ▶ 16-ounce can whole tomatoes
- ▶ 1 pound cooked lentils
- ▶ Salt
- ▶ 1 teaspoon red chile flakes, chopped chiles, or black pepper
- ▶ 3 cups water

Instructions:

Heat the oil and add the cumin seeds. When they pop and make a lot of noise, add the sesame seeds. Wait 5 seconds and add the onions, garlic, and curry leaves. Fresh curry leaves should be torn up and tossed in the oil, while dried curry leaves should be ground up and then added with the other spices.

Add the asafetida and turmeric. Sauté the onions until softened. Drain the tomatoes, reserving the liquid to be used later on. Crush the drained tomatoes with your hands over the onions. Cook on medium-high heat for about 10 minutes. Add the lentils and stir until coated with spices. Season to taste with salt and chiles or pepper. Add the water and the liquid from the can of tomatoes, and simmer for 5 minutes. Serve with brown rice or crusty toasted bread.

This method can be used to make any beans or daal (Indian legume) you like. It won't taste the same, because the beans will all react differently to the flavorings. For a variation in spices, try garam masala or chana masala, added along with the turmeric. Or, if you'd prefer to experiment with your own spices, try adding a pinch of ground cloves and a pinch of cinnamon powder. Both are considered warming spices in Indian medicine. For a very fragrant soup, omit the turmeric and instead use a small pinch of saffron instead, bloomed in a tablespoon of water and added toward the end of the cooking.

Eggplant (Version 1)

Eggplant is one of those things that I am finicky about, because I don't like its texture or mouth feel. I don't like to eat it at all, but I know how to make it because I've watched my mother cooking the stuff, and I know how it's supposed to smell and look in the pot. I haven't had a single complaint. This particular version is quite excellent on bread or over pita bread. The different spices are what give the dish character, because eggplant in itself has no flavor.

Look for the smaller, thinner Japanese eggplants, which have fewer seeds.

 4 to 6

Ingredients:

- ▶ 2 tablespoons peanut oil
- ▶ 1 teaspoon cumin seeds
- ▶ 1 teaspoon mustard seeds
- ▶ 1 teaspoon coriander seeds, lightly crushed
- ▶ 1 tablespoon sesame seeds
- ▶ 1/2 teaspoon fennel seeds, lightly crushed
- ▶ 2 cloves garlic
- ▶ 1 tablespoon minced fresh ginger
- ▶ 2 Japanese eggplants, or 1 regular eggplant, roughly chopped (about 1 pound)
- ▶ 1/2 teaspoon Chinese five-spice powder (star anise, fennel, clove, white pepper, cinnamon)
- ▶ 1/2 teaspoon cinnamon
- ▶ 1/8 teaspoon nutmeg

Instructions:

In a wok or large skillet, heat the oil over high heat. In a small bowl, combine the cumin, mustard, coriander, sesame, and fennel seeds. When the oil is hot, pour in the mixture of seeds. Wait about 30 seconds. When they all begin to pop and crack, add the garlic and ginger, and stir for 1 minute. Add the chopped eggplant, and toss to combine with the spices and oil.

Reduce the heat to medium-low and cover. In a bowl, combine the Chinese five-spice powder, cinnamon, and nutmeg. Stir to combine. In a small cup, collect 1/4 cup of water and set aside. Let the eggplant cook, covered, for about 5 minutes. Open the lid of the pot and pour in the powdered spice blend. Toss to completely combine all the spices, and let the spices cook in the oil for a few more minutes. If you notice the bottom of the wok getting too dry and too many spices sticking, which is likely to happen, just pour in some water and stir to combine, scraping up the bottom of the pot.

Eggplant (Version 2)

🕰 ____4

Ingredients:

- ▶ 5 tablespoons peanut oil
- ▶ 1/2 teaspoon coriander seeds, crushed
- ▶ 1/2 teaspoon cumin seeds
- ▶ 1 medium onion, minced fine
- ▶ 3 cloves garlic, minced fine
- ▶ 1 bay leaf
- ▶ 1 tablespoon grated ginger
- ▶ 1/2 teaspoon curry powder
- ▶ 2 pounds Japanese eggplants, diced
- ▶ 1/2 pound diced tomatoes
- ▶ 1 teaspoon garam masala
- ▶ 5 Thai bird chiles, minced (may be adjusted for your tastes)
- ▶ Salt
- ▶ 1 bunch minced cilantro

Instructions:

Heat the oil in a wide, shallow pan, until a small wisp of smoke escapes. Crush the coriander in a mortar and pestle or in a bag with a rolling pin. Add the coriander and cumin seeds. When the cumin starts to pop, add the onion and garlic. Add the bay leaf. Stir for 1 minute. Add the ginger, curry powder, and eggplant. Cook for 5 more minutes over medium-high heat. Add the tomatoes. Cook for 5 minutes. Add the garam masala. Add the chiles. Cook for 1 more minute. Remove from heat. Sprinkle in salt to taste, add cilantro as a garnish, and stir it through.

This dish is perfect with both flatbread and white rice.

Eggplant Gravy

A simple peanut sauce to accompany the Eggplant Planks on the following page.

Ingredients:

- ▶ Peanut oil
- ▶ 1/4 cup flour
- ▶ 2 cups vegetable stock

Instructions:

Pour the extra oil and spices from the bottom of the baking sheets into a saucepan. Add extra peanut oil until you have 1/4 cup of oil. Sprinkle in the flour to make a roux. When it reaches a blonde color, pour in the vegetable stock. Whisk until thickened, and set aside until needed.

Eggplant Planks

The eggplant planks look so fancy when they're perched atop a bed of basmati rice. I've heard back from some of the testers who were sad to see that there was no leftover oil in the pan after baking. If this is the case, feel free to add in an extra 1 to 2 tablespoons to the gravy recipe. You can scale this recipe up easily. The spices given here are for one large eggplant—if you're using more, just scale up the spices accordingly.

Alternately, some people prefer if the eggplants are cut into disks, rather than planks, because it makes a nice appetizer as well. Feel free to do this, and to experiment with different toppings to serve this as an appetizer.

 6

Ingredients:

- 1 red bell pepper, halved and seeded
- 1 teaspoon cumin seeds
- 1 teaspoon coriander powder
- 1 teaspoon cinnamon
- 1 teaspoon clove powder
- 1 teaspoon turmeric
- 1 teaspoon salt
- 2 tablespoons peanut oil
- 1 large eggplant, sliced lengthwise into planks, 1/2 inch thick
- 1/2 teaspoon ground black pepper or red chile flakes
- Cooked basmati rice

Instructions:

Prepare the Eggplant Gravy (page 71) if you plan to use it. Preheat the oven to 400° F. While preparing the eggplant, roast the red pepper on a baking sheet for about 25 minutes or until the skin is blackened. Take them out and place in a bag or a container with a tight-fitting lid for about 10 minutes. When they're cool enough to handle, remove the skin and pull out the stem and seeds.

Pour cumin, coriander, cinnamon, clove, turmeric, and salt into a spice mill, and grind until very fine. Combine the spice blend and oil to make a loose paste. Rub each plank of eggplant with the spice and oil blend on both sides. Lay the spiced eggplants onto a wire rack. Lay the wire rack onto a baking sheet, and drizzle any remaining oil/spice mixture onto the eggplants. Bake, uncovered, 15 to 20 minutes, or until tender. The roasted red peppers should be ready by the time the eggplants are cooked. Serve each diner with 2 planks of eggplant, 2 slices roasted red pepper, 1/2 cup of cooked basmati rice, and some of the gravy.

Banana Bread

Looking up recipes for banana bread on the Internet is a frustrating experience for me, because they all seem to call for some stupid egg replacer. Let me just clue those people in to a little factoid that vegans the world over have used since...forever: Bananas are used as an egg replacer! To put egg replacer into a recipe that's rife with it seems utterly pointless to this little vegan.

The dough for the bread will be relatively thick. Do not get nervous and decide to deviate from the recipe. That's a bad idea when you're baking. Just go with the (lack of) flow, and move on.

 **6 to 10**

Ingredients:

▶ 3 ripe medium-sized bananas
▶ 2 tablespoons peanut butter
▶ 1/2 teaspoon salt
▶ 1 1/2 teaspoon baking soda
▶ 1 teaspoon vinegar
▶ 1/2 cup water
▶ 3/4 cup sugar
▶ 1/2 cup coarsely chopped nuts
▶ 2 cups flour

Instructions:

Preheat the oven to 350° F. Mash the bananas with the vinegar and the water. Add the peanut butter, salt, baking soda, sugar, and nuts. Stir together to combine. Add the flour, and stir to combine. Pour into a greased dish. I have used a small casserole dish with excellent results. You can try using a loaf pan, but this may leave the center a bit underdone.

Let the bread bake for 1 hour in the oven. Let it cool for 15 minutes before removing from the dish.

Hot Penne

I like my hot penne to be really hot, so 1 tablespoon of chile flakes doesn't nearly cover my needs. I like this with 3 or 4 generous tablespoons of chile flakes. The presentation is simple but beautiful-looking. The red tomatoes with the fresh green parsley and the little red flecks from the chile flakes make the final dish look rather pretty on a clean white plate. Definitely serve this with some kind of steamed or roasted vegetable on the side, because it's fairly plain on its own. Granted, when I make this dish, I keep sneaking more pasta and pretending like I can't see the vegetables.

 4 to 6

Ingredients:

- ▶ 1 pound penne pasta
- ▶ 3 tablespoons olive oil
- ▶ 3 cloves garlic, sliced
- ▶ 1/4 cup oil-packed sun-dried tomatoes, finely diced
- ▶ 1/2 cup minced Italian flat-leaf parsley
- ▶ 1–3 teaspoons chile flakes, according to your taste

Instructions:

Cook pasta.

While the water boils, heat oil in a pan and add garlic. Cook for a few seconds, and then add the tomatoes. You may also want to add some of the oil from the tomato jar. Cook for a few more seconds, and add the parsley and chile flakes. Add pasta to the pan. Toss to combine. Serve hot.

Basic Pasta with Garlic

🕐 **4 to 6**

Ingredients:

- ▶ 6 quarts water
- ▶ 2 cloves garlic, sliced
- ▶ 4 teaspoons of olive oil
- ▶ Red chile flakes to taste
- ▶ 1 pound pasta (such as ziti, penne, or rotini)
- ▶ 2 tablespoons lemon juice (optional)
- ▶ Salt

Instructions:

While you wait for the water to boil, slice your garlic into thin rounds. Heat some olive oil in a pan over medium-high heat and add your garlic. Let it sizzle in the oil until it turns a very light brown (this happens quickly). Remove from the heat, and sprinkle in some red chile flakes. Set this next to your serving plate.

After the pasta is cooked (see the Pasta Cooking Guide, page 18, for time suggestions) drain the pasta and drizzle on the garlic sauce. If you want to, you may add in some lemon juice at this point to brighten up the flavor of the pasta. Sprinkle on a generous amount of salt, adjusting to taste, because the heat of the chiles needs the salt to balance it out and make it pleasant. Toss the pasta to coat it with the oil and garlic mixture.

Steamed but Not Angry Vegetables

This recipe came together after yet another genius managed a thundering failure at steamed vegetables. I was fairly irritated when I put this recipe together, but the taste calmed my tension. I definitely like this one as a base for other flavorings. This is just where you get started—you can always add other things like paprika, chile flakes, or fresh chopped herbs to this, and have a more complex taste. This is what I'd call the bare minimum for steamed vegetables.

Say it with me: There are no boring vegetables, only boring cooks!

    4

Ingredients:

▶ 5 cups water
▶ 1/4 pound baby carrots
▶ 1/4 pound snow peas
▶ 1/4 pound green beans
▶ 2 tablespoons lemon juice
▶ Salt and freshly ground black pepper

Instructions:

In a large stockpot, boil the water. Place a metal colander over the top of the pot. Place the carrots into the bowl of the colander, and cover the pot. Cook for 15 minutes. Add the snow peas and green beans. Cook for an additional 5 to 10 minutes. Remove the vegetables from heat. Toss with lemon. Sprinkle with salt and black pepper to taste and toss. Serve hot.

Basic Roasted Vegetables

In the winter, people often get tired of soup. I put this recipe together as an answer to the endless string of soups you're subjected to during the winter. It will be a nice change.

Don't be fooled by what seem like complicated instructions. This dish is actually easy to put together and provides a lot of options for what to do with your (meager) leftovers. Roasted spiced vegetables always disappear very quickly.

 6 to 10

Ingredients:

- ▶ 1 tablespoon curry powder
- ▶ 1/2 tablespoon garam masala (optional)
- ▶ 4 tablespoons peanut oil
- ▶ 1 pound sweet potato
- ▶ 1 pound butternut squash, peeled and seeded
- ▶ 1 pound parsnips
- ▶ 1 pound carrots
- ▶ 1/2 pound small red radishes

Instructions:

Make a sort of loose paste with the curry powder, garam masala, and the oil, and set it aside while you chop the vegetables. You want the oil to reach above the level of the spices in a thin layer. This is to allow the spices to rest in the oil and, in the end, prevents the spices from burning.

Cut the vegetables into generous pieces roughly the size of the radishes. Mix all the chopped vegetables, and combine with the oil/spices mixture. Make sure that the spices are evenly spread through. Bake in the oven at 350° F until all the vegetables are tender (approximately 45 to 60 minutes). If you're nervous about burning them, loosely cover with aluminum foil before baking and remove it for the last 10 minutes. While your house fills with the smells of the spices, make a pot of basmati rice and toss together a quick green salad of lettuce and cucumber to serve as a counterpoint to the heavy flavors of the vegetables. This also tastes great inside a pita pocket.

The next day, if you simmer leftovers in a little coconut milk and water (1 to 1 ratio) for about 10 minutes, you've got an excellent, creamy soup. The day after that, if you take what little bit of soup is left (because the previous day's soup would have been delicious), and blend it with equal parts olive oil to make a sauce that you can use as a dressing, or just blend the leftovers with a can of chickpeas and a tablespoon of olive oil to make yourself a spread for sandwiches. If any of that spread is leftover the day after that (haha, fat chance), combine it with a splash of lemon juice, and a bit of vinegar for a cool salad dressing.

Cucumber Invasion

I love the flavor of cucumbers with something smoother and darker in the center. Try this with your own favorite spices or seasonings. I call it the Cucumber Invasion, because the little bites of cucumbers are called (in my brain, anyway) cucumber boats.

The neat thing about these little bites is that they look so cute on a platter. Whether you serve them as a side dish at a sit-down dinner or as an appetizer at a party, cucumber boats are bound to be a hit.

 4 to 6

Ingredients:

- ▶ 2 pounds cucumbers (You want a large cucumber)
- ▶ 1/4 pound lentils, cooked
- ▶ 1 teaspoon cumin powder
- ▶ 3 shallots, minced
- ▶ 1 clove garlic, minced
- ▶ 1/4 cup minced cilantro
- ▶ Splash of lemon juice
- ▶ Splash of olive oil
- ▶ Salt and cracked black pepper

Instructions:

Peel the cucumbers and cut in half lengthwise. If you're using small pickling cucumbers, such as Kirby cucumbers, don't worry about peeling off the skin. Remove the seeds with a spoon, making sure to get every last bit of the central pulp out. Toss together the lentils, cumin, shallots, garlic, lemon, olive oil, and salt and pepper to taste. Add the lentil mixture to the hollowed out cucumbers, and sprinkle on pepper. Slice the cucumbers into bite sized pieces. These work well as appetizers. Just make sure that you cut the boats into pieces that are small enough to be eaten in one or two bites.

"The beauty of the way Dino cooks is that there are no set rules. As someone who has had the opportunity to cook with him in person often, he has pushed me into not being afraid to alter my cooking plans at the last minute, or even during the course of cooking the meal. More than once we've started out cooking with one idea in mind, and I've turned around to find him rummaging through my cabinets, where he has found an ingredient I forgot I had, and we've totally changed gears and ended up cooking something entirely different."

—Dana Ballantyne

Chapter 3:
More Complex

You've baked. You've boiled. You've sautéed, simmered, sweated, and soaked. You're familiar with how a vegetable cooking in not enough oil sounds, and you know what smells to look out for so that you don't burn things. You're ready to take things to the next level. While the recipes in this section aren't exactly complicated, they do combine a variety of techniques.

This does not mean, however, that these particular recipes are reserved for some elite cook out there. It does mean that you need to be careful before you embark on these journeys. Read the recipe from start to finish carefully. If you don't know how to make a particular technique work, look up further instructions on the Internet, or call that one friend you've got in your phonebook who knows food. If things get too daunting, remember that the health food store can be an outstanding resource for cooking advice. If you have a decent one locally, swing by there and ask about cooking techniques. Someone is bound to know.

Whatever you do, don't think that because you're not the best cook in the world, you can't make these dishes. They are workable, even for novices. Just take your time, go slowly, and have fun experimenting with your new abilities!

Ⓥ

Tostones

Depending on what part of Latin America one is from, these are called patacones or tostones. These little fried pieces of gold are delicious served piping hot. If you use shortening instead of oil, you'll get a totally different experience; the shortening can get much hotter than oil can, and will give a better crust. Be liberal with the salt and chile. Use canola or peanut oil, so that the second frying won't overheat the oil.

Tostones are the perfect appetizer to any meal, because they're so easy to eat. They're a fair bit more fancy-looking than something like potato chips, but give that same satisfying crunch. If you feel up to it, you can serve them atop a fresh garden salad as croutons, or with some guacamole.

 4

Ingredients:

- ▶ Oil for frying
- ▶ 1 plantain, cut into 1/2-inch disks
- ▶ Salt
- ▶ Chili powder

Instructions:

In a large pot, begin to heat the oil. While the oil is heating, peel the plantains and slice them 1/2 to 3/4 inch thick. If you make them too thin, you'll end up with hard plantains that are difficult to bite through. You want these to be crispy outside and tender inside, so stick with a thick enough plantain. You don't, however, want them too thick.

When the oil has reached 375° F, gently slide in the plantain slices. They will begin to bubble. The best way to tell when they are done is to look around the edges of the slice. If the large bubbles have stopped forming, you're ready to remove it from the oil. This should take roughly 5 to 7 minutes. You want the plantains to be tender at this point.

When cooked, remove the plantain slices from the oil and drain them on a wire rack, standing upright. While they're still hot, liberally sprinkle on some salt. You will now want them to come down to room temperature. While you wait, mix equal parts salt and chili powder as an accompaniment to the plantains when they're ready. Also, heat the oil to 475° F.

Set one of the cooled plantain disks on a flat surface such as a cutting board or counter. Take a large spatula and set the flat of it on top of your plantain. Use the palm of your hand to press down on the spatula to make the plantain into a flat patty. Gently slide the patty into the oil. Continue to flatten and fry the rest of the plantains. When the patties are golden brown, they're ready to serve.

Drain on a wire rack for a few minutes before serving.

Curried Plantains

These are delicious over steamy hot bowls of rice. It's another one of those dishes that my mother came up with when we were younger and were able to find plantains cheaply. Make sure to use green plantains. You can peel them if you want to, but this is optional. You want the plantains to be a fairly small dice, so that they cook more quickly.

 6

Ingredients:

- ▶ 5 tablespoons oil
- ▶ 1 teaspoon cumin seeds
- ▶ 2 teaspoons coriander seeds
- ▶ 2 large plantains, diced
- ▶ 1/4 teaspoon turmeric
- ▶ 1/2 teaspoon chili powder
- ▶ Salt
- ▶ Water (optional)

Instructions:

Heat oil in a wok or skillet over high heat. While you wait for the oil to heat, quickly bash your coriander seeds in a mortar and pestle. If you don't have a mortar and pestle, throw the seeds into a paper bag. Fold the top of the bag to close it shut and run a wine bottle or rolling pin over the bag to crush the seeds.

When the oil is hot, add the cumin seeds. Wait 15 to 30 seconds. The seeds will begin to pop. At that point, add the coriander seeds. Wait about 10 seconds for the popping of the cumin to go down a bit.

Add the plantains and stir to combine them with the spices and oil. Sprinkle in the turmeric, chili powder, and salt. Stir the plantains again, until all the cubes of plantains are yellow from the turmeric.

Turn down the heat to medium-low and cover your wok or skillet. Let it sit like that for about 5 minutes. Open the lid and toss all the ingredients together to redistribute the oil and the spices. If you think that the pan looks too dry for your liking, and you're nervous about burning the spices, feel free to add a little bit of water to the pan and stir it through. You want the dish to be dry, but you also don't want to burn anything!

Continue to cover, let sit, uncover and stir in increments of 5 minutes until the plantains are done. This can take roughly 20 minutes in total.

When the plantains are cooked, serve them as a free-standing side dish, or serve them atop cooked rice for a filling meal.

Manga Thokku (Mango Relish)

This is a South Indian pickle that my mother makes in enormous quantities. Those enormous quantities would be decimated by the time the next mango season rolled around, so she was forever foraging unripe mangoes wherever she got a chance. When I say a large amount, I mean that she'd single-handedly (for a long time, until we all pitched in to help) process multiple kilos of the stuff at one go. Because the green mangoes are grated, you don't really have to worry about soaking them in salt for a week.

> **Pickles and water are mortal enemies!**
>
> When you're making Indian-style pickles, be aware that water is the enemy of good pickles. Water allows mold to grow in the jar and gets things nasty. Make sure that you have absolutely no water in the jars that you store your pickles in. When my mother would store pickles, she would put a sheet of plastic (usually a clean zip-top bag works) over the mouth of the jar before closing the lid tightly. Then, every time one of us would dig into the jar, we would make sure to use only a clean, dry spoon. Then, when closing the jar, the plastic was replaced, and the jar was kept in a cool, dry place at all times.

If you are using very small unripe mangoes, key limes, or cut-up lemons (roughly the size of a golf ball) you can salt them for a week, and follow the rest of the recipe as stated. All you do is put the tiny mangoes, key limes, or lemons into a glass or plastic bowl. You then pour on enough kosher salt to cover all the fruit completely. Yes, this is a lot of salt. I know this. When using this method, don't add salt to the recipe, as the soaked fruit will be plenty salty. Regardless of what you're using, don't bother peeling the mangoes, the key limes, or the lemons. When preserved in salt, then preserved in salt and spices, the flavor is incredible.

I have considerably cut back on the amount of salt for this recipe, because I know there's someone out there who's going to try to eat these like American pickles and then call me screaming. You may want to increase the amount of salt to help preserve it longer. If you do add more salt, it will keep for a much longer time and prevent the growth of bacteria and mold.

+2 weeks fermenting — 4 for a week

Ingredients:

- 1/2 cup oil (peanut, sesame, or canola)
- 2 teaspoon mustard seeds
- 1 unripe medium-sized green mango, grated
- 1/4 cup salt
- 1 teaspoon fenugreek seeds, ground in a spice grinder
- 1 teaspoon turmeric
- 1/8 teaspoon asafetida
- 3 fresh chiles, finely ground

Instructions:

In a wok, or a large skillet, heat the oil over high heat, until a small wisp of smoke escapes the surface. Pour in the mustard seeds. Wait about 30 seconds, until the seeds pop. When the popping subsides a few seconds later, add the grated unripe green mango. Stir to combine in the spices and oil.

Add the salt, fenugreek, turmeric, and asafetida. Stir the grated mango to combine completely. When all of the mango mixture turns yellow, you've stirred it enough. Reduce the heat to as low as it will get. Add the ground chiles to the top, but *do not stir*. Let the mangoes sit, simmering in the heat, until they become a thick paste.

After 15 to 30 minutes, depending on your stove, the mixture will resemble a thick sauce. Turn off the heat, and let it cool to room temperature before storing in a jar. The relish will keep indefinitely. Let it sit 2 weeks before eating.

Bear in mind that water and oil do not mix, so be careful to only use dry spoons when serving the relish, and to leave the jar at room temperature to avoid condensation of water on the inside of the jar. If you happen to get any mold in the relish, just scoop it out, and discard it—the rest of the stuff will not be harmed.

Serve as a spread for bread, as an accompaniment for fresh vegetables, or use it as a kick in your regular food.

Indian Pickles

A pickle in India is something—a vegetable, fruit, etc.—preserved in salt, oil, and spices, not in vinegar. Think of it like a sort of combination pickle/relish/other preserved food. It's meant to be a hot/salty addition, and is meant to be eaten in very small amounts (no more than a teaspoon per meal). They're ideal to take with you on long trips and the like, because they taste great just spread onto some flatbread or stirred into a soup that seems bland. This pickle in particular is not one you'll find elsewhere; it's an amalgam of different pickle recipes that I've liked in the past.

When you make pickles, you're spending a fair bit of time and labor. Double or triple this batch as needed. You really can never have too many pickles. Homemade pickles make excellent gifts for family or friends. They also do well with freshly minted college students. When I went away for several weeks in a residential college program while I was in high school, my mother sent up some pickles with me to save my life. It really came in handy when I was stuck in the middle of nowhere with very bland food to eat.

I remember making pickles with my mother as a child. The whole house would fill up with the smell of the toasting spices and the cooking food. We'd immediately have to try some, even though you're technically supposed to let it sit for a week or so to let the flavors meld properly.

+2 weeks fermenting   **4** for a month

Ingredients:

▶ 1 cup oil

▶ 1 teaspoon mustard seeds

▶ 1 tablespoon sesame seeds

▶ 1 small onion, minced fine

▶ 1 head garlic, minced

▶ 1 tablespoon curry powder

▶ 5 tablespoons salt

▶ 1 pound tomatoes, finely diced

▶ 1 lemon, minced and de-seeded

▶ 1 cup chiles, finely minced

▶ 1 tablespoon chili powder

Instructions:

Heat oil in a wide, shallow pan. Add mustard and sesame seeds, and allow them to pop like mad. Add onions, garlic, curry powder, and 1 tablespoon of the salt. Cook for about 10 minutes, or until the water is mostly evaporated from the onions.

Add the tomatoes and lemons and stir vigorously. Add the rest of the salt. Reduce the heat as low as it will go. Cook 20 minutes. Add the fresh chiles and chili powder. Cook 5 minutes. Cool to room temperature.

Pour the cooked pickles into a jar, and fill the jar about 90 percent full. Pour oil over the pickles to fill out the rest of the jar. Place a sandwich baggie on top. Screw on the lid. Allow the pickles to sit for about 2 weeks before eating.

This is lovely mixed with rice, pasta, or noodles. It also perks up any dish that's too bland. It can be spread onto roti (page 112), with some vegetables for a quick wrap on the go.

Dino Sarma Weierman | Alternative Vegan

Omusubi...Sort Of

The Japanese rice ball (omusubi) usually involves meat or fish. In my version, you're using all plant ingredients. They look pretty laid out on a platter with a sauce. Caveat: these tend to be very bland on their own. Make sure that you serve them with some form of dipping sauce, or people will start to think that vegans eat like invalids. You can use your favorite Asian-style dipping sauce, or use the one I have in the sauces section (page 104).

Unfortunately, it took me a couple of edits to nail this one down properly. The original was rather bland and didn't impress. They looked adorable but tasted kind of dead. I perked them up with the cilantro and ginger. It came out rather nicely.

 6

Ingredients:

- ▶ 1 cup uncooked short-grain brown rice
- ▶ 1 tablespoon oil
- ▶ 1 red bell pepper, finely minced
- ▶ 1 shallot, finely minced
- ▶ 3 red potatoes, boiled and mashed
- ▶ 1 tablespoon ginger, finely grated
- ▶ 1 tablespoon chopped cilantro
- ▶ 2 tablespoons rice wine vinegar
- ▶ 1 teaspoon red chile flakes
- ▶ Up to 1 teaspoon salt (to flavor the rice)
- ▶ 3 tablespoons white sesame seeds
- ▶ 3 tablespoons black sesame seeds

Instructions:

Cook the brown rice (see Rice Cooking Guide, page 21). In a shallow pan, heat the oil, add the bell pepper and shallots, and cook until softened. Remove from heat and let cool down slightly. Mix with the mashed red potatoes. Add the ginger. Shape into teaspoon-sized balls.

Take the rice, and combine with the cilantro, rice wine vinegar, and the chile flakes. Sprinkle in the salt and toss to combine. Taste the rice. If it tastes too bland to you, it's going to need more salt. Without a decent amount of salt, it's going to be horribly bland. This would also be the time to add any extra seasoning that you feel the ball would do well with. Because the bulk of the rice balls is the rice itself, you have to flavor it now.

In the palm of your hand, take some of the rice and press it into a roughly 2-inch disk. Take the small ball of potato mixture and lay it in the center. Bring up the disk around the potato ball, and roll it around in your hand. This should give you about a 1-inch ball.

Combine the black and white sesame seeds together, so that you can see equal amounts of both. Pour the seeds onto a plate. Coat the rice balls with the seed mixture by rolling them around in it. You want them to be lightly coated so that you can see the color contrast between the sesame seeds and the cilantro and chile flakes. Lay them on a wire rack, and spray with sesame or canola oil spray. Bake at 375° F about 20 minutes, or until lightly brown.

Split Pea Croquettes

I came home one night and fried up a batch of frozen falafel I had prepared the week before. My mother took a taste of one and commented that, while the crispy texture was nice, she was displeased with how dry they seemed. The texture wasn't working for her. I explained that you're supposed to eat a falafel combined with a tahini sauce, or in a sandwich, but she wasn't pleased with that answer.

The next week, when I soaked some beans for my next batch of falafel, she convinced me to leave out the chickpeas all together and just use yellow split peas. Once we started to get down to business, we started pitching in grated ingredients that we thought would cut through that dry texture. The first to go in was a large, grated onion. When that worked really well for the first batch, we began adding more and more ingredients to the base recipe. Eventually, we came to the conclusion that while patties of beans taste great, they can be improved infinitely by the addition of vegetables. They become like little portable meals.

The croquettes are not only comforting, they also store really well. If you make up a large batch and freeze the leftovers, they reheat most impressively in the oven. The best-tasting ones are those that aren't perfectly smooth on the outside. The jagged edges and craggy outside allows the croquette to get more crispy, and gives you extra surface area for pockets of sauce to pool in when you dip it into a dipping sauce.

If you want a shortcut to getting all the vegetables prepared, a perfectly reasonable method is to use a basic box grater, and grate everything down. Feel free to add the garlic along with the split peas when you grind them down in the food processor. Avoid using a blender for this recipe, because you want the patties to hold up firmly.

 +8 hours soaking **4 to 6**

Ingredients:

▶ Peanut, canola, or other high-heat oil for deep frying

▶ 1 cup yellow split peas, soaked in water overnight

▶ 1/4 cup shredded cabbage

▶ 1 small onion, minced

▶ 1 small carrot, shredded

▶ 3 cloves garlic, minced

▶ Salt

▶ Water, reserved

Instructions:

Heat the oil 3 inches deep on high heat in a deep-sided pot, wok, or skillet.

Grind the soaked split peas in a food processor until they're the consistency of a grainy hummus. You'll never get them smooth, but you want them to be ground down. If it's not grinding down enough, add a couple of tablespoons of water and keep grinding.

Combine with all the remaining ingredients. Form into rough patties. Drop the patties into the oil, and fry until a dark brown.

This will take roughly 7 minutes per side, depending on how hot your stove gets. Serve with hummus or ketchup.

Note: If you want to pan-fry these, it does work with a healthy dose of oil, heated over medium-high heat, in a wide, shallow skillet.

I Must Be Nuts!

I love roasted nuts, but most of the ones from the store are honey-roasted! This makes me sooo mad! I've developed these to roast on the stovetop in order to avoid trusting the oven to do the deed. The proportions of these nuts are only suggested. As long as you end up with 1 1/2 pounds of nuts, you'll be fine. Use raw nuts for this recipe so that they don't end up overcooked.

 4

Ingredients:

- ▶ 2 tablespoons oil
- ▶ 1 teaspoon mustard seeds
- ▶ 1 tablespoon cumin seeds
- ▶ 1 tablespoon sesame seeds
- ▶ 1/4 pound almonds
- ▶ 1/4 pound hazelnuts
- ▶ 1/2 pound peanuts
- ▶ 1/4 pound cashews
- ▶ 1/4 pound pistachios
- ▶ Salt
- ▶ 2 tablespoons chile flakes

Instructions:

In a large skillet or wok, heat the oil. When the oil is hot, add the mustard seeds. Wait for them to pop. When they begin popping, add the cumin seeds. When both the mustard and cumin seeds are popping and exploding, add the sesame seeds. Once the sesame seeds get lightly browned, add the almonds. Reduce the heat to medium-high. For the next few minutes, make sure you constantly stir the nuts, to prevent burning. Do not let the nuts sit still for more than a minute at a time.

Toss the nuts to combine. Roast them with the spices for about 3 minutes. Add the hazelnuts. Toss the nuts to combine with each other and the spices. Roast together for 3 minutes. Add the peanuts and cashews. Toss to combine, and roast the nuts together for 3 minutes. Add the pistachios. Toss all the nuts together to combine with the spices and nuts. Generously salt the nuts. Roast the nuts together for about 3 more minutes.

Sprinkle in the chile flakes, and turn off the heat. Toss all the ingredients to combine thoroughly. Remove one of the nuts and blow on it to cool it down. Taste it for salt. If you need more, this is the best time to add more.

Flautas

Flautas are so tasty but require a bit of time to make, because the corn tortillas are finicky. If you're really not in the mood for finicky, I promise not to judge you for using flour tortillas, which are ten million times more forgiving. However, I've had friends make these with corn tortillas and report excellent results. They get crispy on the outside, while retaining a puff of fragrant steam on the inside. Just give it a shot with whichever tortilla, and you'll be glad to come back to it.

 4

Ingredients:

- 3 cups water
- 1 large red potato
- 1 cup salsa verde (recipe follows)
- 1 red onion
- 1 red bell pepper
- 8 ounces canned corn, drained
- 2 teaspoon oil
- 1 teaspoon chopped fresh Mexican oregano
- 1/2 teaspoon ground cumin
- Salt
- 8 small corn tortillas
- 15-ounce can black beans, drained
- 2 avocados, thinly sliced
- 6 tablespoons vegetable shortening or Dalda
- Toothpicks (optional)
- 1/4 cup chopped cilantro
- 2 limes

Instructions:

In a small pot, bring the water to a boil. Add the red potato and cover. Return the water to a boil, then reduce to a simmer. Cook for about 30 minutes.

Set your oven or toaster oven to 175° F.

Assemble the salsa verde using the recipe that follows. You want to begin with this part so that it has time to sit around and let the flavors meld. Chop the onions and bell peppers. Drain the corn.

In a saucepan, heat 2 teaspoons of oil. Add your onions, peppers, and the Mexican oregano. Add the cumin powder, and a good pinch of salt. Stir all the vegetables to combine them.

Cook the onions and peppers until they are soft. While they cook, wrap the tortillas in foil, and keep them in the warm oven or toaster. When the onions and peppers are cooked to your liking, drain the can of black beans and stir them into the pan. Feel free to bash the beans around in the pan to mash them up a bit. Cook over low heat for 5 minutes. Turn off the heat, and cover with a lid.

By now, the potato should be cooked. Drain the water from the potato pot, and discard. Give the potatoes a good, quick smash to break them into smaller pieces, using your stirring spoon to avoid burning your hand. Add the potato to the pan with the beans and onions. Using a potato masher, mash the mixture until relatively smooth. Mix while you mash to speed the process along.

Remove the tortillas from the oven, but leave the oven on. Arrange the tortillas, potato and bean mixture, corn, and avocados in front of you in that order, like an assembly line. Take a tortilla in the palm of your hand. In the middle, pile on 2 or 3 generous tablespoons of the potato mixture. Spread the mash on the tortilla shell in one line down the middle.

Take about 1 tablespoon of corn and gently sprinkle it over the potatoes. Put on a slice of avocado. Lay the tortilla aside, open faced, on a cookie sheet and return it to the oven to keep it warm as you assemble the remaining flautas.

In a large high-sided skillet, heat the shortening over medium heat. As the fat begins to melt, remove the cookie sheet with the warmed tortillas from the oven. Carefully roll the tortilla up around the stuffing. If you are using a corn tortilla, you might have some cracking. This is not a problem. Place it seam side down on the cookie sheet. If you want to be on the safe side, secure the rolled up flauta with a toothpick.

You're ready to start frying once the shortening is melted. Pick up one of the flautas, and place it seam side down into the hot fat. If it sizzles and bubbles in the oil, you know that the fat is hot enough to fry the flautas. If it doesn't sizzle and bubble, remove the flauta from the oil and allow it to drain as you wait for the oil to come up to heat. When the shortening is hot enough to sizzle your flautas, slowly lower the flautas into the fat. Let them cook until they are a deep golden brown.

Try not to disturb them too many times, as they need to be left alone to brown. After about 5 minutes, or when the big bubbles start turning clear and subside and they're browned on one side, flip them over with tongs or a spatula to cook on the other side. Brown on both sides. Remove the flautas from the heat and drain in the warm oven for about 30 minutes.

Drain off all but 1 teaspoon of shortening from the skillet. Place the skillet back over high heat. When the oil is hot, pour in the cup of salsa verde. Let the salsa warm through, and remove from the heat.

When it's time to serve, arrange the flautas on a platter, and drizzle on the salsa verde. Sprinkle on the chopped cilantro. Cut the limes into wedges, and serve on the platter, so that each diner can squeeze on some lime as needed.

Salsa Verde

Ingredients:

- 6 tomatillos, husked and quartered
- 1 teaspoon fresh Mexican oregano
- 1 jalapeño, seeded
- 1 bunch green onions
- 1 lime, juiced
- 1 bunch of cilantro, stems discarded

Instructions:

Combine the tomatillos, Mexican oregano, jalapeño, green onions, and lime in a food processor. Pulse until the tomatillos are roughly chopped. Add the cilantro and pulse until combined.

For a hotter salsa verde, add some green Thai bird chiles in addition to the jalapeño.

Bajji

I am a firm believer in the concept that pretty close to anything that you dip in batter and deep-fry will taste good. In the case of bajji, it's usually just potatoes, but I want you to experiment with other ingredients. When I was visiting Chicago, I even managed to use zucchini!

A note on rice flour:

I have had varying reports of success on this recipe. The thing about it is that if you're using rice flour, I would suggest trying to find it at your local Indian store. For whatever reason, the texture of the rice flour found in most health food stores is too coarse for the bajji application, whereas the ones you find in an Indian store will have a finer grain, almost like all-purpose flour. If you have success with the flour you normally buy, then by all means stick with it.

This is one of those dishes that I've managed to teach my mother something about. She used to make her bajji using chickpea flour or all-purpose flour. The bajji was still delicious but would lose crispiness rather quickly. In my version, with the rice flour, the bajji has a chance to get very crispy and stay crispy. If you can't find or afford rice flour, go ahead and use the all-purpose flour. It won't be a huge loss, but it won't be as crispy as with the rice flour.

When you're done frying the bajji, save the oil! It's now been spiced with all those delicious spices you used in the batter. You now have a spiced oil to use in cooking other dishes.

10 to 15

Ingredients:

- ▶ 1 pound potatoes, sliced into disks
- ▶ 1 pound red, green, or orange bell peppers, seeded and sliced into rings
- ▶ 1 pound onions, sliced into disks or rings
- ▶ 1 pound Anaheim chiles, tops removed and seeded
- ▶ 2 cups rice flour, sifted
- ▶ 1 tablespoon curry powder
- ▶ 1 teaspoon cumin
- ▶ 1 tablespoon chili powder
- ▶ 1 tablespoon salt
- ▶ 1/4 teaspoon baking soda
- ▶ 1 3/4 cups ice cold water
- ▶ Oil for frying (in preferred order: peanut, sunflower, safflower, canola)

Instructions:

Prepare all vegetables, and set aside. Combine the flour, spices, salt, and baking soda, and sift together. Slowly pour in water, stirring constantly, until you have a batter that's slightly thinner than pancake batter. You'll want the batter to coat the vegetables, but not coat them thickly. This is a matter of personal preference, and you might want to experiment with the batter slightly thicker than you think it should be. You can add more water if you feel it's too thick, but you can't take it out if you think it's too thin. Be very careful about water content, because adding more flour to the batter throws off the flavorings you've worked to achieve.

Heat the oil to 400° F. Dip the vegetables in the batter. Deep fry in batches, until golden brown. This works best when you have someone helping you. If one person dips the vegetables while the other person babysits the oil, the process runs smoothly.

When golden brown, remove from oil and drain on a wire rack. Serve as soon as possible. This particular dish doesn't need accompaniments, but here's a sauce in case you demand one:

Dipping Sauce

Ingredients:

▶ 1/4 cup oil
▶ 1 tomato, finely diced
▶ 1 tablespoon chili powder
▶ 1/4 cup lemon juice
▶ 2 tablespoons chopped cilantro

Instructions:

Heat oil until very hot. Add tomato. Cook for 10 minutes. Add the chili powder, and cook for about 1 minute. Pour the mixture into a blender with the lemon juice and cilantro, and purée.

Basic Fried Food Sauce

This is really my mother's invention, so I'm crediting her and tweaking it to meet the tastes of a wider audience. I like mine to be screaming hot, but people who are less inclined to call in the fire trucks may adjust this to their own liking.

Ingredients:

▶ 1/4 cup ketchup
▶ Up to 1 tablespoon ground chiles
▶ Up to 1/4 teaspoon salt
▶ Up to 1 tablespoon freshly ground black pepper

Instructions:

Stir to combine. Serve with the pakoras (page 96) as a dipping sauce.

Comforter

What could be better than creamy potatoes and a nice contrast of colors and flavors all wrapped up in flaky, tender puff pastry? Creamy potatoes and a nice contrast of colors and flavors all wrapped up in a flaky, tender puff pastry with gravy! This particular gravy is essentially velouté gravy. I have included it here for quick reference, because this dish is totally not the same without the gravy.

 4

Ingredients:

- ▶ 1 tablespoon vegetable oil
- ▶ 1/4 cup minced shallots
- ▶ 1 clove garlic, minced
- ▶ 1/4 teaspoon cumin powder
- ▶ 1/4 teaspoon coriander powder
- ▶ 1/4 teaspoon turmeric
- ▶ 1 teaspoon curry powder
- ▶ 1 cup finely diced carrots
- ▶ 1 cup finely diced potatoes
- ▶ 1/2 cup green peas
- ▶ 1/2 cup yellow and white corn
- ▶ 1 sheet puff pastry

Sauce/gravy

- ▶ 1 tablespoon flour
- ▶ 1 tablespoon oil
- ▶ 3/4 cup vegetable stock
- ▶ 1/8 cup each white wine and sherry

Instructions:

Heat the oil in a wide, shallow pan over high heat and add the shallots and garlic. Reduce the heat to medium-low and add the cumin, coriander, turmeric, and curry powder. Cook this mixture until shallots and garlic soften.

Increase heat to high. Add carrots and potatoes. Stir the vegetables until all the vegetables are evenly coated in the oil and spices. Decrease heat to medium. Put the lid on your pan, and cook covered until potatoes and carrots are softened. Add peas and corn. Cook for an additional 5 minutes. Remove from heat, and refrigerate.

Split puff pastry into four equal parts. Roll it out until it's 1/8 inch thick. If you're buying premade puff pastry, it is most likely already 1/8 inch thick. Refrigerate.

Start preparing sauce. Add oil to a saucier or shallow pan, and heat over medium-high heat. Sprinkle in flour. Stirring constantly, allow it to cook for 30 seconds, or until light brown. Pour in the vegetable stock and alcohol, whisking constantly. If you're not using alcohol, you may substitute vegetable stock. Bring the mixture to a full boil, then remove from heat. Set the saucier on a cool burner to allow it to drop in temperature more quickly. Turn down the heat to low. If you're using a gas stove, you may replace the pan onto the stove now. If you're using an electric range, wait until the heat of the range has come down to the lower heat. Replace the pan onto the stove, and simmer for about 3 minutes, whisking all the time.

Remove the chilled vegetables and puff pastry from the fridge. Onto the 4 rectangles, arrange the vegetable mixture in the center, leaving about 1 inch all around. Spoon on about 1 tablespoon of the gravy. Lightly spread water around the edges of the puff pastry. Fold the puff pastry in half, to cover the vegetables, and gently press the pastry shut. Cut out small holes onto the top in the middle for venting. Brush the tops of the puff pastry with oil, vegetable shortening, or margarine to facilitate browning. Bake at 375° F until the puff pastry is browned. Let it sit for 20 minutes to cool and to allow the juices to settle.

Winter Rolls

Try this with your own favorite blend. This is another one of those palate cleansers and is a refreshing burst of pure vegetable flavor. These are not like your traditional spring rolls, which are short and thick, these are long and thin. They should be no fatter than the size of two fingers. Depending on where you live, the spring roll wrappers may also be called rice paper.

The vegetables I have listed here are just a start for the recipe. Anything you have lying around the house that you think might taste good would work. If you have some leftover Chinese stir-fry from the night before, you could use that too. This also works very well with rice noodles. As long as you like the flavor of the food before it is wrapped up and fried, you'll be fine.

 4

Ingredients:

- ▶ 12 spring roll wrappers
- ▶ Pot of hot water (not boiling)
- ▶ 4 ounces snow peas, lightly steamed and sliced into long strips
- ▶ 4 ounces carrots, lightly steamed and cut into long, thin sticks
- ▶ 1 cup finely shredded red cabbage, steamed lightly
- ▶ 1/4 cup finely sliced red chiles (optional)

Instructions:

Dip the spring roll wrappers in hot water to soften, and lay flat on a cutting board. On one end of the wrapper, mound small amounts of the vegetables and chiles. Roll it up, making sure to close both ends. Serve with soy sauce with chopped scallions in it.

Kashmiri Biriyani

Decadent yet surprisingly light, this dish is best served with more mildly spiced accompaniments and palate refreshers, such as thinly sliced cucumber, tossed with lemon juice. The flavors in this dish are so complex and delicate that having strongly flavored things in close proximity would be a waste of the ingredients. This is not cheap, but it is worth every penny.

One of the people testing this recipe said that she wishes she could wear the fragrance from the dish as a perfume!

 **6**

Ingredients:

- 1 cup basmati rice, uncooked
- 1 cup sliced lotus root
- 1 cup sliced carrot
- 4 tablespoons vegetable shortening, peanut oil, or other high-heat oil
- 1 tablespoon sesame oil
- 1/4 teaspoon clove, whole
- 1/4 teaspoon black peppercorns, whole
- 1/2 teaspoon cumin, whole
- 3 to 4 green cardamom pods
- 2 sticks cinnamon
- 1/2 teaspoon fennel seeds
- 1/2 teaspoon coriander seeds, gently crushed
- 1/4 cup cashews
- 1/4 cup pistachios
- Pinch of saffron, steeped for 5 minutes in 3 tablespoons hot water

Instructions:

Get the basmati rice cooking first (see Rice Cooking Guide, if needed, page 21).

Slice the lotus root into 1/2-inch disks. Slice the carrots into 1/2-inch disks. Set aside. Heat a wide, shallow pan over high heat. In the pan, melt the shortening, and pour in the sesame oil. You will need this much oil. Do not decrease the amount of oil. When a wisp of smoke escapes the surface of the oil, it is hot enough for the spices to be added.

Add the clove, the whole black peppercorns, cumin, cardamom pods, sticks of cinnamon, fennel seeds, and crushed coriander seeds. When cumin starts to pop in 30 to 45 seconds, pour in the cashews and pistachios.

Reduce the heat to medium. Cook the nuts and spices over the medium heat for 3 to 5 minutes, or until you smell a light nutty smell. Stir constantly to ensure that the nuts get

thoroughly coated in oil and spices, and so that the nuts don't overcook.

Add the carrots. Stir to combine in the oil and spices. Reduce the heat to medium low, and put on the lid. Cook 5 to 8 minutes, until the carrots are half-done. Add the lotus roots, and stir very gently to combine (you want to maintain their appearance). Put the lid back on, cook 10 to 15 minutes. The lotus is going to be a little on the crispy side, so don't worry about this. They just need time to cook.

Remove the pot from the heat and allow it to cool slightly. Add the steeped saffron to the pot. Stir gently to combine. Lay out the rice onto a platter. Evenly coat the rice with the spiced carrot and lotus root combination. With two salad forks, gently toss the rice through the spice and vegetable mixture, being careful not to smash up the rice or break up too many of the delicate, long grains.

Pakora

Pakora is sort of the long-lost cousin of Bajji (page 90). Personally, I prefer Bajji to Pakora, but when you throw cauliflower into the mix, I'm there quite quickly. I'd still prefer to prepare Pakora, because it's a lot less finicky than Bajji. You're not fussed about doing perfectly thin slices of anything, and dipping the little rounds endlessly, while you watch your family devour each one as it comes out of the fat. Again, as with Bajji, these are traditionally made with chickpea flour, but I prefer to use rice flour. Feel free to substitute all-purpose flour, chickpea flour, or whatever flour you have lying around.

 6

Ingredients:

- ▶ 1 head cauliflower
- ▶ 3 tablespoons oil (in order of preference: peanut, sunflower, safflower, canola)
- ▶ 1 teaspoon cumin seeds
- ▶ 1 teaspoon coriander seeds, crushed
- ▶ 1 teaspoon curry powder
- ▶ 1/2 tablespoon salt

Batter
- ▶ 3 cups rice flour
- ▶ 1 teaspoon cayenne pepper
- ▶ 1/2 teaspoon garlic powder
- ▶ 1 teaspoon chili powder
- ▶ 2 1/2 cups water
- ▶ 1 teaspoon sesame seeds
- ▶ 1 teaspoon ajowain seeds (optional)
- ▶ 8 cups oil for frying
- ▶ 5 slices bread

Instructions:

Break up cauliflower into florets. Add the oil to a wide, shallow pan, and allow it to get hot. Crush the coriander seeds in a mortar and pestle, or in a sealed bag with a rolling pin. Add cumin and coriander seeds. When they start to pop, add cauliflower. Sprinkle in the curry powder and salt. Toss to coat. Reduce the heat to medium-high, and continue to stir as needed.

Cook covered roughly 15 minutes, so that the cauliflower is cooked 3/4 of the way through but not softened. If you find the pan getting too smoky, you may add 1 to 2 tablespoons of water and stir it around.

Sift together the flour, cayenne, garlic powder, and chili powder. Add water to the flour. Mix through. It should be the consistency of a loose pancake batter. Add the ajowain seeds and sesame seeds. Stir through. This is your batter mixture.

Allow the cauliflower mixture to cool to room temperature.

Pour the oil into a 1-gallon pot. Heat the oil to 375° F. Dip the florets into the batter, and deep fry until golden brown. Alternately, you may want to just dump the entire amount of cauliflower into the pakora batter, stir everything around to combine it, and drop it by the spoonful into the oil. Drain the pakoras on a wire rack, and serve hot with a sauce that's good with fried foods.

Chapter 4:
Sauce

Sauces are good to know, if for no other reason than you will have a good grasp on how to mask mistakes. When a soup turns out too watery for my liking, I'll often add a bit of gravy to it. If a dish is looking a little oddly colored, a bit of a roux-based sauce will hide any blemishes. With these basic sauces, go ahead and expand your existing repertoire.

Beurre Mani

Traditionally, this is made with butter, which is disgusting and not vegan. The purpose is to have starch suspended in oil that will slowly release into a soup or sauce. Any thing with a beurre mani needs to be cooked for extra time after being incorporated to avoid the raw flour taste. Use these in soups that have long-cooking vegetables that you don't have time to thicken with a roux. Because the base is so easy and quick to make, you can perform food first aid almost immediately. The repeated boiling, alternated with the simmering allows the soup to gradually accept the thickener, get to the full thickening strength, and then allow the thickener to mellow out and let you see roughly how thick the soup will become. Bear in mind that any thickened soup or sauce will get thicker as it cools down.

 4

Ingredients:

- ▶ 1 tablespoon shortening
- ▶ 1 tablespoon flour

Instructions:

Massage the flour and shortening together, kneading the shortening through the flour as well as you can. Make sure they are thoroughly combined, so that the resulting dough ball is tight. Use the beurre mani to thicken soups that are too watery.

Here's how:

- ▶ 1 pot of overly watery soup.
- ▶ 1 recipe's worth of beurre mani, divided into 10 equal parts.

Drop in one of the balls of beurre mani, and stir to combine into the soup. Let the soup come to a full boil. Reduce the heat to a simmer. Stir to combine all the ingredients. If the soup is thickened to the desired thickness, stop now. If not, continue adding extra balls of the beurre mani, and stir again to combine. Bring it to a boil and then lower the heat to a simmer, stirring to combine and to gauge the thickness.

Once the soup has reached its desired thickness, let the soup continue to simmer for an additional 20 to 30 minutes, to cook out the raw flour taste. Taste the soup and check for salt and seasonings. If you need to add additional salt or seasoning, do so now, and let the soup simmer for an additional 5 minutes, to allow the seasonings to permeate.

Roux

A roux is also traditionally made with butter, which should show you how gross traditional cuisines can be. Roux is meant to be a base for sauces, such as gravies, where you want thickness and a lightly roasted flavor. For a sweeter sauce, please use something like a slurry instead. The darker you make your roux, the less it will thicken your sauce or soup. The blonde roux is the most basic one. I use olive oil because it imparts a clean flavor. Use regular all-purpose flour to avoid weird flavors.

Ingredients:

▶ 3 tablespoon olive oil

▶ 3 tablespoon flour

Instructions:

In a wide, shallow skillet, heat the olive oil over medium-high heat. Sprinkle in the flour, ensuring that you have it sprinkled in at an even level. Immediately, with a whisk or a wooden spoon, stir the flour completely through to coat in the oil. Make sure that all the flour is well coated.

Over medium-high heat, continually stir the flour/oil mixture until it reaches a light blond color. Depending on your stove, this can take anywhere from 5 to 10 minutes. Remove the pan from the heat, and reserve until your liquid to make the gravy, sauce, or soup is ready.

Velouté (Gravy)

A velouté is a classic French sauce that involves stock with bones in it. I use vegetable stock to provide superior results. You don't have to use your own homemade vegetable stock; a good quality, low-sodium one should work just fine. Use a white wine or a sherry to avoid overpowering the rest of the velouté.

 6

Ingredients:

▶ 1 cup vegetable stock
▶ 1/2 cup white wine or sherry
▶ 1 recipe roux (page 99)

Instructions:

Place the pan with the roux onto the heat, over high heat. When the flour sizzles, pour in the stock and wine, and whisk. If you don't have wine, you can use more stock instead. Whisk the sauce vigorously until all the lumps are whisked out. Bring the sauce to a full boil, and then reduce the heat to a simmer. Simmer for about 5 minutes, or until the sauce reaches desired thickness. Remove from the heat and serve.

Gravy-Thickened Soup

Ingredients:

▶ 1 pot overly watery soup
▶ 1 recipe of gravy

Instructions:

In the last 5 minutes of cooking, pour gravy into the soup pot. Bring the soup to a full boil, then reduce it to a simmer. Let it simmer for 5 minutes in total. The soup will get even thicker as it cools.

Slurry

A slurry is for when you want a clear, shiny sauce. They are popular in Chinese cuisine. When you go to an Asian restaurant and see a shiny, glazed-looking sauce over the food, the chef used a slurry to make that glaze. You may use arrowroot, kudzu, tapioca starch, or cornstarch in slurry types of dishes. Do not allow a slurry dish to come to a boil, as the starches will get overcooked and won't thicken properly. If you see bubbles, the heat is too high.

Slurry-based sauces can be a lot of fun to experiment with. Try using pineapple juice or orange juice instead of straight water, and you'll have a sweet glaze. Throw some lemon onto the finished dish, and you'll have a sweet and sour sauce. Toss that sweet and sour sauce with sautéed or steamed vegetables, and you've got a cool-looking, Asian-looking dish, ready to go over rice or noodles.

 4

Ingredients:

▶ 1 tablespoon starch
▶ 1 cup plus 3 tablespoons water.

Instructions:

In a saucepan, heat 1 cup of water to a bare simmer. Do not allow bubbles to form, as this means that the water is too hot. In a bowl, combine 3 tablespoons of water and cornstarch. Mix well to form a loose batter. Pour in a few tablespoons of the hot water. Stir vigorously to combine. Pour in a few more tablespoons of the water. Stir to combine. This is your slurry.

Pour the slurry into the remaining water in the pot. Stir to combine, and simmer it for about 3 minutes. Turn off the heat and remove the pot from the stove to cool. It will come down to room temperature in minutes.

Spicy Soup Cream

If you've ever made a soup that looks like it needs a little something more, you've found the perfect recipe here. The problem with cooking with peanut butter, almond butter, cashew butter, or any of the other nut butters is that they're too sweet. Use tahini and you end up with bitter undertones. Commercial nut milks are far too thin for making a soup creamier, and they lack the actual nuts themselves, which lend an interesting and pleasurable texture.

Try this both at the stove and at the table. You can add the soup's cream toward the end of a recipe, or have a small bowl of it at the table for people to blend into their own bowls. This is quite a versatile recipe, and can be used as a creamy salad dressing as well. You can use my recipe for roasted nuts (page 87) or use your favorite commercial mixed nuts. If you're using a commercial variety, add a teaspoon of cumin powder to the recipe.

 4

Ingredients:

- ▶ 1 cup roasted nuts
- ▶ 1 clove garlic
- ▶ 1 1/2 to 2 cups water
- ▶ Salt

Instructions:

In a blender, add the nuts, garlic, and 1 cup of the water. Begin pulsing in short bursts, to get the nuts coarsely ground. Pour in an additional 1/2 cup of water, and pulse for longer periods. If the sauce looks too thick and the blender cannot handle it anymore, add more water and continue to pulse. In the last stages, when the sauce looks smooth, let the blender grind the sauce at full speed until it's completely smooth.

Orange-Hugged Sauce

Jenna made a comment in the VeganFreak Radio podcast about yuppie names for food that make the white middle-class folk salivate. She referred to "cilantro-kissed black beans" and my brain followed the line to the next logical step after kissing, which is what inspired this title.

 **3**lbs. veggies

Ingredients:

▶ 4 cups orange juice

▶ 1 tablespoon lemon juice

▶ 2 tablespoons ginger, grated

▶ 2 tablespoons sesame oil

▶ 1 teaspoon sesame seeds

Instructions:

Bring the orange and lemon juices to a rolling boil. Reduce the heat to a gentle simmer and allow the juices to decrease to 1/4 the original volume (1 cup). Add the ginger and simmer for 5 more minutes. Add sesame oil and whisk vigorously. Pour the sauce into a blender with the sesame seeds, and blend on high for 1 minute.

This sauce is excellent on grilled food: grilled eggplant, grilled zucchini, grilled portabella mushrooms, or pretty much any vegetable you grill. You can even use it as a marinade, but it's perfect as a sauce. Try it sauce poured over fresh berries for a dessert that bites back. This is also pretty good on salad. If adding to a salad, try adding some chopped cilantro.

Asia Sauce
(for Asian-type appetizers)

I put this sauce together to go over the Omusubi (page 85), because the rice balls are fairly plain on their own. You can use it with other Asian-style appetizers that you're serving with rather good results.

 4 to 6

Ingredients:

- ▶ 1 tablespoon rice wine vinegar
- ▶ 1 tablespoon tamari or soy sauce
- ▶ 1 tablespoon grated ginger
- ▶ 1 tablespoon scallions, chopped
- ▶ 3 tablespoons sesame oil
- ▶ Salt and freshly ground black pepper
- ▶ 1 tablespoon kimchee (optional)
- ▶ 1 clove garlic (optional)

Instructions:

In a small bowl, combine the vinegar, tamari, ginger, scallions, sesame oil, and salt and pepper to taste, and whisk vigorously to make a vinaigrette. If it seems a little bland, add the kimchee as well. If it's still too bland for you, add some extra ginger. If it's still a bit tame, increase the pepper, mince the garlic clove, and blend those in. If you're still feeling underwhelmed, you've got no taste buds left. For a slightly creamier-looking sauce, you can add all the ingredients to a blender and blend on high until it's combined. This particular recipe should be able to serve 2 to 4, depending on the amount of sauce each person likes.

"Providing more of an outline than a formal recipe is the best way for vegans to learn to cook. With Dino's guidance you know what you're making will be good and he lets you tune into your intuition to make it great."

—Kris

Chapter 5:
Dished to Impress

These dishes, while not complicated, do look and taste impressive as if you had spent multiple hours on making them. Serve these to those guests who are not used to vegan food as a sort of invitation to try something new. I've included dishes from when I was growing up and new ones that I developed on my own. In both cases, the food is so different from the run-of-the-mill that the diner will begin to develop the understanding that vegan food is not only delicious—it's diverse as well!

Ⓥ

Asian Pesto Tomatoes

This is the perfect appetizer to serve as a refreshing palate-cleanser between the heavier snacks you'll be serving alongside them. If you want a more complete dish, you can just serve this over pasta, and it tastes outstanding. Use a short pasta, such as farfalle.

 10

Ingredients:

- ▶ 1/2 cup sesame oil
- ▶ 1 clove garlic
- ▶ 1 tablespoon salt
- ▶ 1/2 teaspoon black pepper
- ▶ 1 tablespoon chopped cilantro
- ▶ 3 ounces cashews
- ▶ Splash of rice wine vinegar
- ▶ 1 pound cherry tomatoes
- ▶ Italian flat-leaf parsley, leaves separated from the stems.
- ▶ Endive leaves

Instructions:

Pour oil, garlic, salt, and pepper into a blender. Blend on high until the garlic is smooth. Add the cilantro. Pulse two or three times until the sauce becomes green. Add cashews. Pulse until the cashews are chopped. Add just enough rice wine vinegar to loosen the pesto until it becomes possible to pour (roughly 2 tablespoons). Pour out and chill.

Cut off the tops of the tomatoes, and scoop out a centimeter or so of the meat with a grapefruit spoon or a melon baller or the tip of a paring knife. Fill the vacated space with Asian pesto. Chill until ready to serve.

Because of the sheer riot of colors, you want to serve this on a white plate with some pretty greens that you find pleasing, such as curly parsley or kale. If you serve it in the bowl part of an endive leaf, you'll be able to have a sort of salad on the go.

Black-Eyed Peas Daal

Black-eyed peas are common in both the American and Indian south. They are creamy and have a distinct flavor all their own that you won't find in other beans. I'd describe the texture as somewhere between a lentil and a black bean. It cooks up much softer than a black bean, but stays together better than lentils do. The ease of making this dish builds with time, as you get used to making this sort of thing. Once you've got the recipe in your head, the making of it is fairly simple.

 **10**

Ingredients:

▶ 1 pound dry black-eyed peas, cooked, with cooking liquid reserved

▶ 4 tablespoons oil

▶ 1 tablespoon mustard seeds

▶ 2 tablespoons cumin seeds

▶ Large handful of curry leaves

▶ 2 cups chopped onion

▶ Generous sprinkling of salt

▶ 2 teaspoons turmeric

▶ 5 plum tomatoes, chopped

Instructions:

Begin with a large stockpot. Heat the oil over high heat. When the oil is hot enough that you see it get less viscous when you move the pot around, immediately add the mustard seeds and wait 30 seconds for popping to begin. Add the cumin seeds when the popping subsides. Strip the curry leaves off their stalks, tear them in half, add them, and step back while they explode. Add the onions immediately and stir to combine. Sprinkle in the salt and turmeric. Stir to combine.

Reduce the heat to medium-low, and cover the pot. Walk away for about 5 minutes. Start chopping your tomatoes. After 5 minutes, check the pot and stir the onions around to redistribute the spices and oil. If they're ready, you can increase the heat to high. If they aren't ready, give the onions another 5 to 10 minutes, until they're softened.

When the onions get soft, increase heat to high and add the chopped tomatoes. Stir to coat in the oil and sprinkle in a little more salt to draw out the water. Stir until all the oil and spices are mixed thoroughly. Reduce the heat to low. Put on the lid to the pot. Set a timer for 15 minutes.

Drain the beans. In a separate pot, boil the reserved bean liquid to reduce it. You'll leave it at a medium boil (over medium heat) until you're ready for it. When 15 minutes have passed for the tomatoes, check the pot and see that they're fairly well broken down, and slightly browned around the edges. This is good.

Pour in the beans and stir to combine. When completely coated in the tomato mixture, pour back in the bean cooking liquid from the other pot. Stir to combine. Increase the heat to high. Wait for it to come to a full, rolling boil. Boil the beans for about 5 minutes. Remove from heat and serve over brown rice.

Sambhar

Sambhar is essentially a wet curry. It's excellent as a side dish for dosa, vada, or idli. It's really spicy, and the tamarind paste gives it a dark, earthy flavor that cannot be matched by anything else. That mix of hot, slightly salty, and sour, along with the grounded texture of the daal, is quite an interesting sensation.

 **10 to 15**

Ingredients:

▶ 1 1/2 cups dry toor daal or yellow split peas

▶ 6 cups (for legumes) plus 2 cups water

▶ 3 tablespoons oil (in preferred order: peanut, sunflower, safflower, canola)

▶ 1/2 tablespoon black mustard seeds

▶ 1/2 tablespoon cumin seeds

▶ 1/2 tablespoon coriander seeds, crushed

▶ Dash of asafetida (optional)

▶ 1/2 pound onions, roughly chopped

▶ 1 teaspoon salt

▶ 1 tablespoon fenugreek powder (lightly roast fenugreek seeds over medium heat until light brown and grind when cool)

▶ 1 teaspoon turmeric

▶ 1 teaspoon coriander powder

▶ 1 potato, coarsely cubed

▶ 1/2 pound carrots, coarsely chopped

▶ 1 eggplant, coarsely chopped

▶ 1 tomato, coarsely chopped

▶ 10 stalks curry leaves (optional)

▶ 5 green chiles, chopped

▶ 1 tablespoon chili powder

▶ 2 tablespoons tamarind paste (if using concentrate, use 1 level teaspoon)

▶ 1 cup chopped cilantro leaves (garnish)

Instructions:

Boil the toor daal or split yellow peas for about 30 minutes in a separate pot. *Save the cooking liquid!* Heat the oil in a giant stockpot, and add the black mustard seeds. When they begin to pop, add the cumin seeds. Allow those to pop, and add the coriander seeds.

Sprinkle in a dash of asafetida.

Add the onions. Blend the salt, fenugreek powder, turmeric, and coriander in a small bowl and add this mixture to the stockpot. Sauté over high heat until the onions are lightly browned. This should take anywhere from 5 to 10 minutes. Stir it well to allow all the flavors to combine properly.

Add the potatoes and carrots, and sauté until cooked through. This should take around 15 minutes and is a fairly involved process. To expedite the process, turn down the heat to medium and put the lid on. Every 5 minutes or so, come in and stir the ingredients to avoid sticking to the pot too much. If there is some sticking, it's fine, because when you add water, it'll release all those delicious flavors.

Add the eggplant, tomato, toor daal, and about 3 cups of the cooking liquid. Cook with the oil and allow it to heat through. Strip the curry leaves from their stalks, chop them, and cook for 5 minutes. Add the water and the chiles. Bring to a full boil. Add the chili powder and the tamarind paste. Bring back to full boil, and cook for 5 minutes. When it is done, remove from the heat and scatter on the cilantro leaves for garnish and flavor.

Rasam

This one's my own version, because I find the original version to be kind of weak in flavor. My mother used to make huge batches of rasam and use it whenever one of us had an upset stomach. We'd eat it over mushy white rice as a soup, and it was so comforting on rumbling tummies.

 **10**

Ingredients:

Rasam powder

▶ 1 tablespoon dry toor daal or yellow split peas

▶ 5 to 6 dry red chiles

▶ 1/2 tablespoon cumin seeds

▶ 1 tablespoon coriander seeds

▶ 1 teaspoon peppercorns

▶ 5 stalks curry leaves

▶ Roast all the spices in a small pan, and grind in a coffee grinder when cool

Rasam

▶ 1 cup dry yellow split peas

▶ 1 tablespoon oil

▶ 1 tablespoon black mustard seeds

▶ Tiny dash asafetida

▶ 1/4 cup curry leaves

▶ 1 pound tomatoes

▶ 1–4 teaspoon freshly ground black pepper, to taste

▶ 2 tablespoons tamarind paste (if using concentrate, use 1 level teaspoon)

▶ 1 gallon water

▶ Cup minced cilantro leaves (garnish)

Instructions:

Boil the split peas in a separate pot for 20 minutes. Heat oil in a pot, add mustard seeds and allow them to pop. Add a dash of asafetida. Tear the curry leaves in half and add them. Add the tomatoes, and sprinkle on salt. Cook for about 5 minutes. Add the black pepper, the rasam powder, and the tamarind paste. Add the water. Bring to a full boil, and keep it boiling for 15 minutes. When cooked, sprinkle on cilantro for garnish. Serve over mushy rice.

Spinach, Indian Style

Served with a basmati rice, this fragrant spinach dish will make mouths water before even hitting the table. I was always shocked at how my friends in the United States treated spinach. I'd see it in a gray mass that was limp and smelled vile. Why did it smell bad? Because the lot of it was just boiled and served straight up. There wasn't any flavoring added. There were no spices. It was horrible stuff.

Fortunately, my mother loves spinach and knows just how to make it. I have modified her recipe and the recipe that I've eaten in various Indian restaurants over the years.

 6

Ingredients:

- 1 tablespoon peanut oil
- 1 teaspoon sesame oil
- 1 teaspoon cumin seeds
- 1 teaspoon coriander seeds, crushed
- 1 tablespoon sesame seeds
- 1 large Spanish onion, diced fine
- 2 pounds spinach (yes, you'll need that much—this stuff goes *fast*)

In a bowl, combine these spices:

- 1 teaspoon garam masala
- 1/2 teaspoon kosher salt
- 1 teaspoon ground black pepper
- 1 teaspoon chili powder
- Grating of fresh nutmeg
- 5 cloves garlic, finely minced

Instructions:

Heat the oils in a wok or large, shallow pan on high heat. Add in the cumin seeds. When they begin to pop (up to a minute), add the coriander seeds. These won't need to pop, so only wait 5 seconds. Add the sesame seeds. Wait until they pop (up to a minute). Add onions and sauté until softened.

Add the spinach and blend of spices listed above. Stir to coat. This is a fair bit of greenery to work with, and it's mostly spread out instead of being concentrated. You will have to add the spinach in waves. Wait for the first batch wilt down, then add some more. That batch will wilt a bit, and you add some more. Depending on the size of your pot, this may take anywhere from 3 to 5 batches. It's perfectly fine. When most of the spinach has wilted down, add the garlic. Cook 3 more minutes, or until all spinach is wilted.

Serve over a bed of basmati rice. Accompany with roasted vegetables and a fresh garden salad for a complete meal. Can also be served with Indian flatbread, such as roti (page 112) or naan.

Tomato Rice

This is one of my favorite rice dishes of all time. It's funny, because Mom didn't make this as much as her friend did. We had professed love for that kind soul's version, which Mom took to mean that she was saved from having to bother making it anymore. Every time we'd visit this friend in any context, the dear woman would think of my sister and me, and cook up a batch especially for us to eat.

Of course she made enough for everyone to eat, but that minor detail never got in the way of both of us feeling really special. If you ever do come into contact with children who like a particular dish that you make, be sure to do it as often as possible, because it's a memory they'll cherish for their entire lives. I know I still think about my mom's friend to this day, and it's been years since we've seen her.

 6

Ingredients:

- ▶ 3 cups uncooked long-grain rice
- ▶ 2 tablespoons peanut oil
- ▶ 1 teaspoon sesame oil
- ▶ 1 teaspoon black mustard seeds
- ▶ 1/2 teaspoon coriander seeds, crushed
- ▶ Dash of asafetida
- ▶ 1 stalk curry leaves
- ▶ 1 large Spanish onion, diced
- ▶ 2 cloves garlic, minced
- ▶ Salt
- ▶ 1/4 teaspoon curry powder
- ▶ 2 pounds tomatoes, finely diced
- ▶ 1 tablespoon crushed black pepper

Instructions:

Cook the rice ahead of time. Spread the cooked rice onto a wide, shallow serving dish.

If you have nonstick pans, this would be the time to use them. Add both oils to the pan and heat well. Add the black mustard and coriander.

When the spices pop (up to a minute), add the asafetida. Tear the curry leaves in half and add them. Immediately add the onions and garlic. Sprinkle on about 1/2 teaspoon of salt, so the water in the onions evaporates faster. Add the curry powder. Stir constantly to avoid burning.

When the onions have shrunken down in size, add the tomatoes and immediately turn down the heat to medium. Add in an additional 1/2 teaspoon of salt to facilitate water evaporation. Stir the tomatoes and cook on medium for about 3 minutes. Reduce the heat to low and gently simmer the tomatoes until the water evaporates enough, and the tomatoes break down enough, that you have reduced it by half. Add pepper. This isn't an exact science, and you've got some wiggle room, so it's OK if your first batch or two turns out a little on the watery side.

When done, pour the mixture over the rice and mix gently to avoid mashing the rice. Serve at room temperature, but not cold. If it feels a little too cold, you can sprinkle on some water and warm it in the microwave for about 1 minute per serving. Serve as a main dish, with a side salad as a counterpoint to the heat of this dish.

Roti

Roti is ideal for travel, because it keeps so well. I like adding spices to mine, because then I can eat it all by itself. The spices also help preserve the roti for long trips. Omit the spices for a clean canvas to work on. Add ground herbs for a different effect. Use garam masala or curry powder for a wholly different taste. This will work perfectly well as a plain roti if you leave out the spices. The spices, however, give it a kick that complements any meal.

Freeze it!

Yes, you may have your roti disks made ahead of time. Freezing roti is an easy way to avoid going through all the work and effort of making roti every single time you have a yen for flatbread.

All you have to do is get it rolled out and cooked. Stack it with sheets of parchment paper between each roti to prevent sticking, and wrap your stacks of roti (I like to wrap mine in stacks of ten), and freeze them.

When you're traveling, make a large stack of roti, and keep it in one of those insulated boxes. Pack a box of daal, Dry-Cooked Chickpeas (page 52), Indian Roasted Potatoes (page 68), pickles (page 84), or anything you think would go well with a flatbread. You'll find yourself slowly sneaking more and more of the roti along with whatever accompaniment you brought. This particular version that I have here is quite good all by itself.

 6 to 10

Ingredients:

- ▶ 2 1/2 cups whole wheat flour
- ▶ 3 tablespoons wheat germ
- ▶ 1 teaspoon salt
- ▶ 1 teaspoon ground black pepper
- ▶ 1 teaspoon coriander powder
- ▶ 1 teaspoon cumin powder
- ▶ 1/4 teaspoon cinnamon
- ▶ 1/4 teaspoon clove powder
- ▶ A grating of nutmeg
- ▶ 1/4 teaspoon freshly ground cardamom
- ▶ 1 cup plus 3 tablespoons warm water
- ▶ Flour for dusting
- ▶ Oil for spreading and to prevent drying out

Instructions:

Mix all dry ingredients together. Add water, 1/4 cup at a time, and knead the resulting dough. Use flour to dust your counter if the dough ball feels too sticky. You don't want it to stick to your hands.

Divide the dough into balls about 2 tablespoons in size. Take each lump of dough and roll it into a tight little ball. You may want to use a little oil when rolling the ball to prevent the ball from sticking to your hands and to prevent the dough from getting dried out.

Toss each ball in flour, and generously dust your counter. Roll each ball into a disk with a rolling pin, liberally dusting all the way. You want disks about 1/8 inch thick. They should be lightly coated with flour. Lay them all out in a single layer on your counter, avoiding overlap.

On medium heat, preheat a heavy-bottomed skillet (cast iron is ideal). Gently lay the disk of dough onto the skillet. When little bubbles appear on the surface of the roti, flip the disk over. Wait about 30 seconds and flip it over once more. With a kitchen towel that's been rolled up, gently press down all over the roti to encourage it to puff. Once your puff is achieved, keep it in an insulated container. Spread a little bit of oil over the top to make the roti moist.

Fill the roti with your favorite roasted or dry-cooked vegetable, and roll up for a quick snack on the go. Spread on some agave nectar and brown sugar to an unsalted, plain roti for a sweet snack. Top off with fruit and fold in half for an easy-to-eat dessert. Make the dough with an extra healthy dose of spices to have a stand-alone roti. Try it smeared with roasted garlic and ground sun-dried tomatoes. Use it like a tortilla shell for your favorite cooked beans, rice, and vegetable mixture.

Puri

In its simplicity, puri is (in my opinion) the easiest flatbread to crank out en masse. If you really don't give a fuck how the thing looks, do what my mom does: roll out the dough in one fell swoop, cut into equally sized sections (with a pizza cutter), and fry the sections. Rolling out each one separately is a pain in the butt, but it does make a nice presentation.

 6

Ingredients:

▶ 1 cup whole wheat flour
▶ Up to 1/2 cup water
▶ Peanut or canola oil for frying

Instructions:

Combine flour and water until the consistency of wonder bread: doughy, pasty, that sort of thing. It should be able to hold its shape, and you should be able to roll it out. Separate the dough into 8 to 10 equal parts. Roll the lumps of dough into little balls. Liberally dust your work surface with flour and roll out the balls into disks. Each should be about as thick as

a CD. Pour oil into a wok (ideal) or deep pot and heat to 375° F. You want the oil to be fairly deep, because the puri is going to puff up like a balloon. Around 6 inches deep should suffice.

When frying puri, bear in mind that the goal is to achieve a puff. The dough takes little to no time to cook, so the technique is important. Gently slide the disk of dough into the hot oil. It will sink to the bottom, then try to float back up. Gently take your slotted spoon and push down on the disk to dunk it under the hot oil. Continue to do this until it becomes puffed. Then flip over the puri to cook on the opposite side. When lightly golden brown, remove from the oil and drain on a wire rack (paper towels just make it swim in its own fat—ew).

Coconut Rice

This is a dish that my mom used to serve up on those days when we'd get fresh coconuts from the market and she didn't particularly feel like spending hours in the kitchen. It's simple because it's meant to be a quick dish.

It's best if you use freshly grated coconut, but not imperative. However, do not use sweetened coconut, because the sugar preserves it and allows them to sell you an inferior, less fresh product. If you're feeling sort of lazy, remove the coconut meat from the shell and throw it into the blender with about a cup of water. Blend on high until finely grated. Then, squeeze out the liquid and save it. This is coconut milk, and it's worth its weight in gold! It's perfect as an addition to soups when the soup is almost done, as it allows you to add lemon to the soup, and still have a creamy flavor in there. Then use the coconut that you've drained in this recipe.

This is not to be confused with tender coconut, which comes in a coconut with the husk still on it and has a slightly gelatinous texture. You want mature coconut, that's thick and white. There is a lot of water in the coconut, and this tastes good to drink all by itself.

 10

Ingredients:

- ▶ 3 1/2 cups cooked rice
- ▶ 1 1/2 tablespoons peanut or canola oil
- ▶ 1/4 teaspoon cumin seed
- ▶ 1/4 teaspoon black mustard seed
- ▶ 1/2 teaspoon coriander seeds, crushed
- ▶ Tiny dash of asafetida (optional)
- ▶ 1 stalk curry leaves (if available)
- ▶ 1/2 cup whole cashews, unsalted (optional)
- ▶ 1 whole chile, sliced in half (scrape out seeds for a milder flavor)
- ▶ 1 coconut, grated (1 1/2 cups)

Instructions:

When the rice is done, dump out onto a wide, shallow serving dish to come down to room temperature.

Heat your oil in a wide, shallow pan or a wok. When hot, add the cumin, mustard, and coriander seeds. When they start to crackle and pop, add the dash of asafetida. Tear the curry leaves in half, add them, and let them pop.

Throw in the cashews and roast for a little less than a minute. Add the chile. Add the coconut, and roast over medium-high heat, stirring constantly. When the coconut turns light brown in color, turn off the heat, and pour the mixture over the room-temperature rice.

Using salad serving forks, gently toss the mixture through the rice, being careful not to break up the long fragrant grains of basmati rice. Serve immediately as a main dish, with some kind of steamed or grilled vegetables. You may add salt to the coconuts while roasting them, but it's not completely necessary.

Saffron Rice

My friend Dana had some saffron in the house, along with some basmati rice that we'd just bought earlier that day. We had finished cooking a particularly large and somewhat exhausting meal. I didn't have the patience for a proper biriyani, but I still wanted a rice dish with saffron in it. Granted, the saffron would not have gone to waste, because the stuff is gold to me, but that's not the point. What we ended up with was a light, delicately perfumed dish that went well with the heavily spiced foods we made that night. It's been a favorite of ours ever since.

 6

Ingredients:

▶ 2 cups uncooked basmati rice
▶ 1/2 teaspoon saffron threads (usually one small packet)
▶ 1/4 cup hot water
▶ 1 cup unsalted raw cashews, roughly chopped

Instructions:

As the rice is cooking (see Rice Cooking Guide if needed, page 21) heat the water so that it's very hot but not boiling. Microwaving it in a coffee mug works great for this. Dump the saffron threads in the hot water and set the mug aside to steep.

Lightly roast the cashews in a pan over medium heat until they're slightly browned. When the rice is done, mix in the saffron-water carefully so as not to mangle the rice, and then add the cashews.

Chapter 6:
Easy Peasy

These are those recipes that you crank out quickly when you're running late but need some food. These are the things you cook when you're still learning to cook. These are those recipes without which any cookbook would seem incomplete.

Garlic Bread

I've seen people pay exorbitant rates for "Texas toast," which is essentially giant slabs of bread with partially hydrogenated vegetable oil. Often times, these margarines contain whey, casein, or any number of other disgusting dairy products that we most assuredly will do well to avoid like the plague. On top of that, they've been sitting there in the packaging for who knows how long!

However, garlic bread is a passion for me, because the marriage between the hot steamy bread—crusty on the outside and fluffy soft on the inside—and the sharp, pungent garlic and little bursts of salt is a pleasure to be experienced, not merely a food to be eaten. Without the humble loaf of garlic bread, most meals seem empty and pointless. Why did you even bother to roll out of bed if you don't have a warm, crusty baguette waiting for you?

Do not relegate yourself to substandard garlic bread substitutes made by corporations just salivating at the thought of sneaking yet another evil ingredient onto your dinner plate. Fight the power! Eat your own garlic bread! And now that you think I'm a raving lunatic, onward to the recipe.

 4 to 6

Ingredients:

- 1 crusty baguette
- 1 clove of garlic, finely minced or crushed
- 1 clove of garlic, cut in half lengthwise
- Salt
- 3 tablespoons olive oil

Instructions:

Preheat oven to 350° F. Cut the bread almost in half lengthwise. You want there to be a bit of a "hinge" on the bread. In a small saucepan, heat the garlic and oil over a gentle flame, until the garlic just sizzles. While you await the sizzle, take the halves of garlic you have and rub them all over the baguette. This imparts a garlic flavor to the outside of the bread.

When the garlic in the pot is sizzling, remove it from the stove. Spoon the garlic-oil mixture into the "pocket" you've created in your baguette. If you got overzealous with the knife, and didn't leave a hinge, it's OK. Just spoon the garlic oil mixture onto the bottom half of the baguette. Then, firmly press on the top loaf and handle it that way. If you have a spray bottle with water, spray on some water. If you don't, lightly sprinkle some water over the loaf. If you do still have your hinge, close the "door" of the baguette and wrap it in foil.

Bake at 350° F for 5 to 7 minutes. You just want the loaf warmed through.

Herb Garlic Croutons

I tried making my own croutons because I wanted a salad and didn't want to go to the store. When I was finished composing my salad, I arranged the croutons in a little pile on the edge of my plate. I flipped on the TV to watch Finding Nemo, my favorite movie of all time, and distractedly munched through my pile of greens. I was in veg-out heaven. When it got to the part when Nemo finds out about the evil niece Darla, I realized that I forgot to eat the croutons with the salad. I still wanted a little something to take that last lingering edge of hunger away, so I just munched on the croutons, and was shocked by how delicious they were all by themselves!

Who needs potato crisps when you've got toasty little croutons? I happily devoured the remaining croutons in what seemed to be the space of one second flat, and have been making them as a snack for myself and my mother ever since. Be sure to make more than you think you'll need, because they go fast.

 6

Ingredients:

- ▶ 1 baguette
- ▶ 1 clove garlic, sliced in half lengthwise
- ▶ 2 tablespoons Italian seasoning, or more for a large baguette
- ▶ Olive oil cooking spray
- ▶ Salt

Instructions:

Preheat oven to 350° F. Take a garlic half and rub it onto your baguette. This adds a gentle backdrop of garlic to the croutons that won't dominate the other flavors. Use the whole clove—you never want to waste yummy garlic!

Slice the baguette into 1/2-inch rounds. If it is a fat loaf, simply slice the loaf into half lengthwise. Slice each half lengthwise again, so that you have four large sticks. Slice those sticks into 1/2-inch pieces.

Arrange the bread on a cookie sheet so that it's in a single layer. Rub the Italian seasoning in between your palms to release the herbs' oils and sprinkle evenly over the bread. Give the bread a light mist of the cooking spray. Sprinkle on salt to taste. Bake until golden brown.

The thing about making croutons is that you want them to be cooked but not brittle. There should still be a little bit of softness in the center of the crouton. Start the oven off at 350° F, and bake them for about 5 minutes. Remove the baking sheet from the oven. Pick up one crouton with tongs, and blow on it to cool it down. Pop it into your mouth and eat it. If it's still too soft, increase the temperature of the oven to 375° F, and bake a couple more minutes. Test another one like you did before. Still not ready? Let it go a little longer. It'll involve some tweaking until you're able to come up with an approximate time for how long your oven takes.

Plain Hummus

In most hummus that you'll buy or make, you'll have all sorts of extra bells and whistles. You can add different aromatics, vegetables, olives, garlic, flavorings that run the gamut from the basic, like salt and pepper, all the way to the fancy, such as minced truffles. This, however, is a recipe for what makes a hummus a hummus. These sorts of things are really not negotiable when making hummus. From this base hummus, you can begin to experiment with different bells and whistles. If you use canned chickpeas, omit the water from the recipe and don't drain the chickpeas.

 6 to 10

Ingredients:

▶ 1 pound cooked chickpeas, drained (roughly 2 cups)

▶ 1/4 cup olive oil

▶ 1/4 cup tahini

▶ 1/4 cup of lime or lemon juice

▶ 1 clove garlic

▶ 1 teaspoon cumin powder

▶ 1 teaspoon salt

▶ Parsley, chopped

Instructions:

In the bowl of a food processor, add the chickpeas, olive oil, tahini, lime or lemon, garlic, cumin, and salt. Pulse in short bursts for about a minute. The chickpeas should be broken up fairly well, but will be rather thick. Add in about 1/2 cup of water and pulse for another 15 seconds, in short bursts. Open the food processor, and taste the hummus. If you feel like it needs salt, sprinkle in some additional salt. If the hummus looks too thick, you may want to add more water. Replace the lid of the food processor and blend. If the paste still looks too thick, drizzle in more water, 1/4 cup at a time, until it looks like the consistency you want.

When the hummus is smooth, set on a platter. Sprinkle with parsley and lightly drizzle with olive oil. This is just a personal preference, but when I make my hummus, I prefer to serve the pita bread toasted lightly. It makes for a really nice textural variation.

If you don't have a food processor: You can still make delicious hummus. In most Latin American stores, you can find a large wooden mortar and pestle. Find the largest one you can, and pound the ingredients in the mortar and pestle. This also makes a fun party dish! All you do is place all the ingredients in the bowl of the mortar and pestle, and have your guests pound out fresh hummus right there on the table. If you don't have the money for a mortar and pestle (even though you can snag one for a few dollars), use a potato masher. If you've managed to lose your potato masher, get all the ingredients into a high-sided pot, and stir everything around vigorously with a large wooden spoon. Hummus is a delicacy that nobody should have to do without.

Black Olive & Truffle Oil Hummus

 6 to 10

Ingredients:

- ▶ 1 pound cooked chickpeas, drained
- ▶ 1/4 cup olive oil
- ▶ 1/4 teaspoon ground cumin
- ▶ 1/4 cup crushed garlic
- ▶ 1/4 cup tahini
- ▶ Splash of lemon juice
- ▶ Generous pinch of salt
- ▶ 1/4 teaspoon chili powder
- ▶ 1 can black olives, chopped
- ▶ 1 teaspoon white truffle oil
- ▶ Parsley, chopped

Instructions:

Sauté chickpeas in olive oil until lightly browned. Add cumin powder and crushed garlic, and toss through until combined. Blend until smooth in a food processor with tahini, lemon, the olive oil in the pan, salt, and chili powder. When smooth, remove from food processor and mix in half the can of olives and the white truffle oil. Put hummus on a large platter so that it's 1 inch thick. Make 3 slight indentations that span the length of the hummus in the center.

Drizzle olive oil into the middle one, and sprinkle a mixture of parsley and chopped olives. *Very* lightly sprinkle chili powder to taste over the olive/parsley mixture.

Roasted Red Pepper Hummus

⏰ **6 to 10**

Ingredients:

- 2 large red bell peppers
- Salt
- 1/2 cup olive oil
- 1 pound cooked chickpeas, drained
- 1 teaspoon cumin powder
- 3 or 4 cloves garlic, crushed
- 1/4 cup tahini
- 1/4 cup lemon juice
- Parsley, chopped

Instructions:

Preheat the oven to 400° F. Cut the bell peppers in half lengthwise and remove the seeds and stems. On the inside of the red peppers, sprinkle in some salt and drizzle a few drops of olive oil. Rub the salt and olive oil into the insides of the bell pepper. Lay the halves of bell pepper skin side up on a baking sheet. When the oven comes to the proper heat, put the peppers into the oven. Set the timer to 10 minutes.

In a wide, shallow pan, heat the oil over medium-high heat. Add the chickpeas, cumin, garlic, and a good sprinkling of salt. Cook the chickpeas in olive oil along with the cumin powder and garlic 10 to 15 minutes, or until lightly browned. You may stir every couple of minutes to redistribute the flavors.

When the timer goes off, check the peppers. If the skin isn't black yet, allow it to bake for another 5 minutes. When the skin is completely blackened, remove from the oven and put a large bowl over the peppers. The beans should be ready by now. Set the beans and covered peppers aside for roughly 10 minutes.

Set up your food processor, juice your lemon, and chop the parsley. In the bowl of the food processor, add your cooked chickpeas, tahini, and lemon juice. Set aside.

By now, the peppers should be ready. Remove your bowl. The peppers should be soft and pliable, and the skin should easily rub off with a paper towel or kitchen towel. Do *not* wash under water to remove every last bit of blackened skin. If a few pieces remain, it's not a problem. They add to the roasted flavor. Set aside the peppers for now.

Pulse the food processor four or five times until the ingredients are roughly chopped. Open the food processor, taste the mixture for salt, and add more as needed. If it tastes a little too salty, add some additional tahini and double the amount of lemon. If it's too dry, add some water or lemon juice as your own taste dictates. Pulse a few more times. Taste again. If it tastes right, blend until smooth. Add the red pepper.

Pulse until the red peppers are evenly combined. Spread on large platter so that hummus is 1 inch thick, sprinkle with chopped parsley, and drizzle lightly with olive oil. Serve with wedges of tomato, wedges of lemon, and a basket of warmed pita bread.

Variations:

Lower fat: instead of using all that olive oil, give the pan a blast with nonstick cooking spray or an oil mister. Stir in · cup of water with the lemon juice.

Hummus Canapés

This is another one of those recipes that just looks really pretty on a plain white plate. The color isn't a sharp contrast, but it is nice enough that a "busy" plate with a lot of patterns on it will detract from the dish's beauty. Try serving this on a stainless steel or silver plate. Or, for an interesting and beautiful presentation, serve them atop a mirror. The reflections and the bright lights shining around the little canapés will give an impressive-looking presentation.

🕐 **10 to 15**

Ingredients:

- ▶ 1 pound cucumbers, sliced into disks
- ▶ Your favorite small crackers
- ▶ 8 ounces hummus
- ▶ 4 ounces black olives, sliced
- ▶ Small bunch of dill
- ▶ Olive oil (optional)

Instructions:

Lay 2 overlapping cucumber disks onto a cracker. Spread hummus onto the cucumber disks. Lay on a slice of olive. Top with a little sprig of dill. You may also drizzle on a tiny bit of olive oil.

Variations:

In lieu of, or in addition to the olive, you may also want to add:

- ▶ A thin slice of sautéed mushroom;
- ▶ A grape tomato;
- ▶ A curl of carrot (sliced from a carrot with a vegetable peeler);
- ▶ A thin slice of red chile;
- ▶ A small piece of red bell pepper;
- ▶ A "sword" of chive, laid on top;
- ▶ A leaf of flat-leaf parsley;
- ▶ A tiny sprinkle of lemon zest;

Hummus Bites

 10 to 15

Ingredients:

- ▶ 1 tablespoon olive oil
- ▶ 1 teaspoon cumin seeds
- ▶ 1 tablespoon sesame seeds
- ▶ 8 to 12 ounces chickpeas, drained and rinsed (1 can)
- ▶ 1 teaspoon salt (adjust up or down to personal preference)
- ▶ 1/4 cup water or lemon juice
- ▶ 1 teaspoon paprika
- ▶ 1 tablespoon tahini (optional)
- ▶ 20 to 30 mini pita breads, crackers, or bread disks

Instructions:

In a wide shallow skillet or wok, heat the olive oil over medium-high heat. Sprinkle in the cumin seeds. Wait 30 to 60 seconds, until they begin to explode and pop. Sprinkle in the sesame seeds. Add the chickpeas and salt, and toss to combine all ingredients evenly. Toss continuously for 3 to 5 minutes, or until the chickpeas are golden brown.

Pour in the water or lemon juice, paprika, and tahini, and stir the chickpeas to combine.

Increase the heat to high and toss the ingredients in the skillet until the liquid mostly evaporates and the chickpeas have the creamy coating of the tahini. Turn off the heat, but leave the skillet on the stove.

Method 1: Mini Pita

Cut open the pita bread via a small slit measuring about 1 1/2 inches along the side seam of the mini pita bread. Stuff with 2 to 3 chickpeas, depending on what you can fit. Serve on a large platter as appetizers.

Method 2: Crackers

Between two fingers, smoosh 1 to 2 chickpeas. Lay the smooshed chickpeas on top of a cracker. Sprinkle on a couple of the sesame seeds and a couple of the cumin seeds. Serve on a platter as appetizers.

Method 3: Toast points, bread disks

Using your thumb and forefinger, split 2 to 3 chickpeas in half horizontally along their natural seam, and arrange the halves on top of the toast point or bread disk. Serve on a platter as appetizers.

Vizza

Vegan pizza often involves ingredients that are either omni substitutes, or stuff that's canned, frozen, or not so easy to build. This one's quick, easy, and tasty. If you're not a fan of nightshade or prefer not to eat raw tomato, this works wonderfully with thinly sliced red bliss potatoes, thinly sliced olives, or even thinly sliced cucumber. If you don't have lavash, you can also use a flour tortilla.

What I like about this recipe is that it is eminently customizable. If the variations I have presented do not look appetizing to you, make up your own! The important thing is to stack up ingredients that will taste good with the hummus.

 1

Ingredients:

- ▶ 1 sheet of lavash
- ▶ 2 tablespoons hummus
- ▶ 1 plum tomato
- ▶ 1 tablespoon chopped parsley
- ▶ Splash of lemon
- ▶ Salt

Instructions:

Spread hummus onto the lavash. Slice your tomato into thin slices. Arrange them onto the lavash in concentric circles. Sprinkle on some lemon and parsley and salt. Cut the vizza into 8 slices, and eat like regular pizza.

Level 2 Vizza:

Onto the regular vizza, add sliced Kalamata olives and marinated artichokes.

Level 3 Vizza:

Bake Level 2 for 5 minutes at 475° F.

Level 4 Vizza:

Drizzle on Vizza Oil (1 teaspoon olive oil mixed with truffle oil).

Level 5 Vizza:

Slice some portabella mushrooms as thinly as you can get them. Toss with thyme and rosemary and some olive oil. Bake the mushrooms at 450° F for about 10 minutes, so that they get crisp. Lay them onto the vizza and serve as normal.

Level 6 Vizza:

When making your hummus, peel the chickpeas. Once peeled, press the beans through a strainer. With a large wooden spoon, vigorously mix in 4 tablespoons of extra virgin olive oil. Grind in some white pepper. Thinly slice some garlic, and bake at 400° F until dried out. Grind in a spice grinder. Sprinkle into the bean mixture and stir in completely. Use this instead of regular hummus.

Lavash Buddy

Lavash is like a soft matza, but with leavenings and fat. I found some kosher, pareve lavash at a dollar store near my house. I've been having fun making different dishes with it. This morning, I'm horribly late to work. I'm typing this on the bus while I'm silently swearing under my breath. I had to take my lunch, because I'm meeting a friend for lunch and I'm not sure where she'll want to go. Thank goodness I made hummus last night, because I had something ready to bang out by the time I needed to head out the door. Here's what I did.

 1

Ingredients:

- ▶ 1/4 cup hummus
- ▶ 2 sheets lavash
- ▶ 1 Persian cucumber, or 2 Kirby cucumbers

Instructions:

Spread hummus onto lavash. Slice the cucumbers in half lengthwise, then make the halves into strips. Lay half the cucumbers onto one lavash sheet and roll up tightly. Lay the rest of the cucumbers onto the other sheet and roll that one up as well. Slice each roll in half at a steep angle. Pack tightly into a box. Take a small baggie of hummus for dipping. Run out the door. When you get to work, pop it into the fridge.

Dino Sarma Weierman | Alternative Vegan

Pita Not Pizza

🔔 ⌣ 1

Ingredients:

▶ 1 pita bread

▶ 2 tablespoons hummus

▶ 1 red potato, sliced into very thin rounds

▶ 1 red onion, sliced into thin rounds

▶ 1 tomato, sliced into thin rounds

▶ 1 clove of garlic, minced

▶ 1/4 teaspoon cumin powder

▶ Olive oil

Instructions:

Spread hummus onto the pita bread. Lay down one slice of potato. Next to it, overlapping most of the potato, lay down the onion slices. Then, next to the onion, overlapping most of the onion, lay down the tomato. Alternate this way until the pita bread is covered. Sprinkle on the minced garlic and the cumin powder, and lightly drizzle with the olive oil. Bake at 350° F for about 15 minutes, or until the vegetables are browned.

Pita Pockets

Although the traditional falafel with tahini is divine, I'll leave that up to the professionals. I like my homemade pita bread to have other ingredients that I find interesting to me. I don't cut the pita in half to make two little half-moon looking pockets. I prefer to make an opening in one end about a few fingers wide, so I can tuck in my ingredients. Try your own favorite combinations for an interesting and varied menu. Or, have a party where guests can choose from piles of delicious looking ingredients, and make their own.

Red ingredients make for a nice, rich flavor.

 1

Ingredients:

▶ 1 pita bread

▶ 1 small beet, roasted and thinly sliced

▶ 3 sun-dried tomatoes packed in oil

▶ 1 plum, or Roma tomato, thinly sliced

▶ 1 whole red bell pepper, seeded and roasted

▶ 2 red onions, sliced

▶ 1 red chile, roasted

▶ 2 tablespoons Italian flat-leaf parsley

▶ 2 or 3 basil leaves

▶ Salt and freshly ground black pepper

Instructions:

Slice the pita bread open along the seam, about halfway. Layer on the roasted beets on the bottom. Then stack on the tomatoes, peppers, onion, chile, and herbs. Complete it with 2 or 3 grinds of black pepper and a sprinkle of salt.

Dino Sarma Weierman | Alternative Vegan

"Heart-y" and Hearty

Although I'm specifying couscous, this is equally delicious with steamed millet, quinoa, or rice, if that's what you have. In fact, I freely substitute millet for couscous when I'm feeding gluten-free folk. If you treat millet just like pasta, you'll end up with fat, fluffy grains by the end of cooking, which you can quickly drain, rinse, and have ready to roll in a short time.

4 to 6

Ingredients:

- ▶ 1 tablespoon olive oil
- ▶ 2 cloves of garlic, finely minced
- ▶ 1/4 teaspoon cumin powder
- ▶ 1 medium red onion, chopped
- ▶ 2 pounds beefsteak tomatoes
- ▶ 1/4 cup minced mint
- ▶ 1/4 cup minced cilantro
- ▶ 1/2 cup lemon or lime juice (use freshly squeezed key limes, if available)
- ▶ Salt
- ▶ 1 package or 1 cup uncooked couscous, prepared (follow package instructions) in vegetable stock instead of water

Instructions:

Heat the oil in a wide, shallow pan and add the garlic and onions. Sauté until the onions are soft. Add the tomatoes and toss through very quickly. Only allow it to stay on for about a minute. Remove from heat. Toss with the chopped herbs. Mix the lemon and lime juices, and add just enough salt for the entire dish.

On a plate, spread out your couscous to form a sort of bed. Spoon the tomato mixture over the top. While delicious as a side dish, it can also be served over toasted bread with a garden salad to make a really interesting and filling lunch.

Okra Buried Treasure

The purpose of getting the oil in such an amount that you're virtually deep frying it is so that you reduce the slimy texture that okra is so infamous for. The tomatoes, in their acidic goodness, cut through further sliminess. Meanwhile, okra is healthy for you and is rich in B and C vitamins, and in essential minerals. This is a good way to get people who aren't usually fans of okra to eat the stuff. I still hate okra, though.

I'm calling it buried treasure, because you're cutting the okra into thin, round disks, that are shaped like little okra coins. This dish tastes fine on its own, or over bread or rice.

 4 to 6

Ingredients:

- ▶ 1/3 cup peanut or other high heat-tolerant oil
- ▶ 1 teaspoon cumin seeds
- ▶ 1 teaspoon sesame seeds
- ▶ 2 stalks curry leaves, ripped
- ▶ 1 pound okra, cut into coins
- ▶ 1 teaspoon salt
- ▶ 2 cloves garlic, minced
- ▶ 1 large tomato, chopped

Instructions:

Preheat a wide skillet on medium heat. Slice the okra into thin, coin-shaped rounds. Discard the stems. Pour oil into the skillet, and turn the heat to high. When the oil is hot, pour in the sesame seeds and cumin seeds. After they start popping, throw in the curry leaves and step back, as they will explode loudly. Immediately add the okra to the skillet. Arrange the okra medallions in such a way that they are almost submerged in the oil, and sprinkle in the salt. Do not stir. This almost deep frying method allows the okra's mucilaginous texture to be suppressed or even removed. When the okra begins to brown lightly (this can take up to 5 minutes, depending on how hot your skillet is), add the garlic and tomato to the pan, and stir to combine in the oil. Cook for 3 more minutes, or until the tomato has broken down slightly. If the pan looks too dried out, you may add some water, as needed.

Collard Greens

This recipe works fine with any greens. Kale, beet or radish greens, mizuna, or whatever you can get your hands on. The point is that you're combining greens with lots of different spices, herbs, and aromatics. Also, you're pulsing them in the food processor so they're diced. They're less threatening that way, because they'll easily mix into rice or pasta without being a chore to chew through.

 4 to 6

Ingredients:

▶ 3 tablespoons peanut oil

▶ 1 tablespoon yellow mustard seeds

▶ 3 stalks curry leaves

▶ 1 cup onion, diced

▶ 2 cloves garlic, minced

▶ 1 teaspoon minced sage or 1/2 tablespoon dried

▶ 1 teaspoon turmeric

▶ 1 tablespoon chopped fresh thyme or 1/2 tablespoon dried

▶ 1 tablespoon dried marjoram

▶ 1 tablespoon dried basil

▶ 1 tablespoon coriander powder

▶ 1 tablespoon paprika

▶ Salt

▶ 1 bunch or bag collard greens, diced in a food processor

▶ 2 cups walnuts, roughly chopped

▶ Up to 1/2 cup water, reserved

Instructions:

In a wide, shallow pan, heat the oil over high heat. When a little wisp of smoke rises from the surface of the oil, sprinkle in the mustard seeds. Wait for about 30 seconds. When they begin to explode, tear the curry leaves and throw them in. Immediately add the onion and garlic and stir to coat in the oil. Add the sage, turmeric, thyme, marjoram, basil, coriander, paprika, and a few dashes of salt.

Stir the spices and the onions in the oil for about 5 minutes, or until the onions are translucent. Pour in all the collard greens into your pot. Since they're minced so finely, you don't have to add them in batches if your pan is big enough. Add the nuts. Toss through to coat in the oil and spices and onions and garlic..

Stir-fry the collard greens for around 10 minutes, or until the greens get brighter. About halfway through, you might notice some crusty bits forming in the pan, and some of the greens sticking. This is perfectly normal and may be combated with the addition of up to 1/2 cup of water. This will avoid burned bits in the final dish and will allow the collards to get steamed slightly—and cook faster, so watch out. Most if not all of the water should evaporate off by the time you're done.

Serve over a bed of hot rice or pasta, or in between slices of bread as sandwiches.

Dino Sammich

So called because if Dino were to make himself a sandwich, this is indeed what he would put into it. I won't talk about myself in the third person after this one little lapse.

 1 to 2

Ingredients:

▶ 1 pita bread

▶ 1 teaspoon stone ground mustard

▶ 2 tablespoons hummus

▶ 1 Kirby cucumber, thinly sliced lengthwise

▶ 1 plum tomato, thinly sliced

▶ 1 shallot, thinly sliced

▶ 1/4 cup Kalamata olives, smashed and pitted

▶ 1/4 teaspoon cumin powder

▶ 1/2 teaspoon chili powder

▶ 1 teaspoon lemon juice

▶ Olive oil

Instructions:

Slice the pita bread in half along the seam to make two rounds of pita bread. On one side, spread the mustard. Atop this, spread half the hummus. Layer on the vegetables. Smash the Kalamata olives until they sit relatively flat. Lay them down on top. Sprinkle on the cumin, chili powder, and lemon juice. Drizzle with olive oil. Spread hummus on the second round of pita. Lay it on top of the sandwich. Slice in half. You may tuck this into another pita half to avoid falling vegetables, but I think that it makes it all too bready.

California Veg Wrap

I made this particular recipe to have enough fillings for 2 wraps, because leaving behind a half of a cucumber is annoying. If you do not have lavash, simply use a regular wheat tortilla wrapper.

 2 to 4

Ingredients:

▶ 2 lavash sheets or wheat tortillas

▶ 3 tablespoons hummus

▶ 1 romaine lettuce heart

▶ 1 English cucumber, seeded and cut into long, thin slices

▶ 2 plum tomatoes, thinly sliced lengthwise

▶ 2 tablespoons alfalfa sprouts

▶ Handful of spinach

▶ Sliced black olives

▶ Sliced marinated artichoke hearts

▶ Salt and freshly ground black pepper

▶ Chili powder

Instructions:

Spread hummus over each lavash sheet. On one edge of the sheet, layer the ingredients in the order listed. Heat a griddle, and spray with cooking spray. Roll up as desired, making sure to fold in the left and right sides of the wrap before rolling up, to keep the wrap closed. Lay down the wrap onto the hot griddle and press down with a spatula. Cook 1 minute, then flip to cook the other side. Press down this side. Remove from heat, and allow it to settle. Wrap in tin foil, and you're ready to go! Refrigerate if you're keeping it for more than 1/2 hour.

Variations:

▶ Thinly sliced zucchini or eggplant, roasted and spread with olive oil

▶ Thin slices of avocado

▶ Pitted olives, sliced

▶ Roasted garlic cloves

▶ Thin strips of carrot

▶ Snow peas, lightly steamed

▶ Your favorite pickle, diced and sprinkled on

▶ Sprinkle of sunflower seeds

Jackfruit Granité

A granité is essentially flavored shaved ice. I've made this dish to be a cooling, calming end to a fiery meal. You will most likely end up using canned jackfruit if you live outside of the regions where it grows, because it can get extremely expensive unless it grows locally. If you're not a fan of jackfruit, feel free to use pineapple, carambola (star fruit), or oranges.

 4

Ingredients:

▶ 1/2 pound jackfruit
▶ 2 cups water
▶ Fresh mint for garnish

Instructions:

Purée the jackfruit and water in a blender until silken smooth. Strain. Pour into a cookie sheet, and freeze. Every hour, go in with a fork, and break up the ice crystals to make tiny shards, until all the liquid is frozen. Serve in a chilled martini glass, with a sprig of mint.

Pomegranate & Wine Slushy

4 to 6

Ingredients:

▶ 1/2 cup pomegranate juice
▶ 1/2 cup pinot grigio or other white wine
▶ 2 tablespoons sugar
▶ Dash of cinnamon
▶ Dash of nutmeg
▶ 2 cups frozen strawberries or cherries
▶ 6 ice cubes

Instructions:

Over medium heat, simmer the pomegranate juice, wine, sugar, cinnamon and nutmeg down until it reduces down to half of its original volume (1/2 cup). Pour the juice and wine mixture into a blender along with the berries and ice, and blend until smooth. Spoon the mixture into wine glasses and chill in the freezer for 15 minutes.

Peanut Butter Banana Smoothie

Ever had one of those mornings when you need something 5 minutes ago, because you're about to miss your bus/carpool/traffic jam avoidance? This is so fast to put together that I can do it even during crunch time. If you make enough for the others in the carpool, they won't be annoyed at the extra couple of seconds you took to bring on breakfast. For whatever reason, bananas that have been ground in the blender tend to be extremely sweet. If yours end up being as sweet as mine, grind them with more ice to dilute them a bit. Also, the liquid amounts here are merely suggestions. You may want to adjust them to your own liking.

If you find yourself running low on peanut butter, feel free to substitute any other nut butter. If you're running low on all of those, try a small handful of nuts. This works with other juices as well. Apple, mango, apricot, or white grape juice would work just fine, as well. The purpose of the orange juice is to give a slightly sour kick.

To remove peanut butter from your spoon, just use another spoon (or your finger) to swipe it off. Do not (as certain people in an unnamed restaurant do) stand there with the peanut butter on the spoon, forever tapping away at the edge of the blender. You'll manage to irritate everyone in the vicinity of your kitchen, and you'll make this thing take much longer than it needs. For shame.

 1

Ingredients:

▶ 1 medium banana
▶ 2 tablespoons peanut butter
▶ 1 cup water
▶ Handful of ice
▶ 1/4 cup orange juice

Instructions:

Combine ingredients in a blender in the order listed. You may want more or less ice, depending on whether or not your bananas are frozen. Blend on high speed until everything is smooth and consistently blended.

Strawberry's Dream

If you can't find vegan graham crackers, just use a slice of bread with a little cinnamon on it. Just toast it for longer, so that the bread gets crispy.

 1

Ingredients:

- ▶ 2 strawberries
- ▶ 1 vegan graham cracker square
- ▶ Dark chocolate
- ▶ Sprig of mint for garnish

Instructions:

Thinly slice your strawberries and lay on top of your graham cracker square in a circle, overlapping the slices. Shave some chocolate on top with a vegetable peeler. Pop into a toaster oven for about 30 seconds at 350° F. Garnish with mint, and enjoy.

Poached Pears in Mulled Wine

This is a dish I created for a friend of mine who was getting married. Her caterer had no clue what to serve after the dinner, and she wasn't about to spend a small fortune on soy ice cream or something along those lines. She wanted something easy to make in quantity with ingredients that the caterer would have on hand. If you don't drink alcohol, thin out some concord grape juice with a little water and use that instead.

 2

Ingredients:

- ▶ 1 star anise
- ▶ 1 stick cinnamon
- ▶ 5 cloves
- ▶ 1 green cardamom pod
- ▶ 2 cups red or white wine
- ▶ 1 pear, peeled, sliced in half lengthwise, and cored

Instructions:

Gently poach the pears in the wine and the spices until wine has reduced by half. When the pears are cooked, remove them from the heat, and chill in the fridge. Reduce the wine to a thick syrup. If it isn't thickening fast enough, sugar may be used to facilitate thickening. Serve each diner half a pear with a few drops of the sauce.

Brandy Mandarin

This is one of those desserts that rounds out a nice long dinner. You can use it as an appetizer, but be careful about how much you serve!

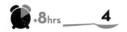 **+8hrs** _____ **4**

Ingredients:

- ▶ 1/4 cup brandy or amaretto
- ▶ 2 tablespoons sugar
- ▶ 1 star anise
- ▶ 1 small can mandarin orange sections, drained

Instructions:

Put the anise seed in a small pot. Over the anise seed, pour in brandy. Bring the brandy to a bare simmer. Pour in the sugar, and heat and stir until the sugar is melted. Pour the brandy syrup over the orange sections. Macerate (let soak) in the fridge overnight. Cover tightly if you have many things in the fridge. Serve chilled with your favorite fresh fruits.

Chilly Martini

It's good, I swear. I personally like my martini to be very dry, so I use a spray bottle to get my vermouth in my glass. If you don't have the vermouth in a spray bottle, measure out the 1/8 teaspoon, because much more than that and your drink is destroyed.

⏰ _____ **1**

Ingredients:

- ▶ 1 ounce vodka
- ▶ 1 red chile, sliced 3/4 of the way in half lengthwise
- ▶ 1 cup cranberry juice cocktail, chilled
- ▶ Dry vermouth in a spray bottle, or 1/8 teaspoon (optional)

Instructions:

Pour the vodka over the chile, and allow it to sit for about 10 minutes. Pour in the cranberry juice and stir to combine. Remove the chile, and perch on the edge of a martini glass. Spray in 1 or 2 sprays of vermouth into the glass. If you don't have vermouth, omit this step. Pour the vodka and juice mixture into the glass. Serve.

Special Edition Coffee

I personally love my coffee black, but you're welcome to splash in some vegan milk if you'd like. However, since this the coffee already has a complex flavor profile, you can be adventurous and try it without creamer. It's worth the effort.

🕐 **4 to 6**

Ingredients:

▶ 1 pot AA Arabica coffee

▶ 6 tablespoons water, boiling

▶ 3 tablespoons cocoa powder

▶ 6 tablespoons sugar in the raw

▶ 1 tablespoon panela (evaporated unrefined cane juice)

▶ 1 1/2 tablespoons cinnamon

▶ Zest of one orange

▶ Pinch of salt

Instructions:

Start the coffee brewing. Boil the water and mix in the cocoa powder to dissolve. Mix in the sugars, cinnamon, orange zest, and salt. (Salt *really* brings out the flavor in chocolate.) When the coffee is brewed, stir your mixture into the pot. Strain it through a fine strainer and pour into prewarmed cups to serve.

Index

About
Dino Sarma Weierman

Dino is a talented chef living in New York City with his adored (and adoring) husband, Stephen. He works for a small vegan restaurant in downtown Manhattan, both in and out of the kitchen. He teaches private cooking classes, maintains a vegan food blog, and updates his cooking podcast whenever the time manifests itself and he can remember to do so. Between work, home, and friends, his life is spent (for the most part) in the kitchen, creating food for all manner of people.

He's been cooking for years, under the tutelage of his mother, then later cooking shows on TV, and finally, under his boss at his workplace. During all that time, he's made careful observations of how the experts do things, then promptly adapts the methods to his own tastes, as he encourages everyone else to do.

As always, he can be found with either a book in his hand, puttering around on the Internet, listening to podcasts on the subway, watching cooking videos on popular video sharing sites, or chatting in IRC to his friends. Although he lives in a fourth-floor walkup, working in a restaurant has added a good twenty pounds to his once-svelte frame. Since his husband proposed to him after five years of unofficial marriage when marriage equality passed in New York, Dino is really not bothered about the more of him that there is to love.

About PM Press:

PM Press was founded at the end of 2007 by a small collection of folks with decades of publishing, media, and organizing experience. PM Press co-conspirators have published and distributed hundreds of books, pamphlets, CDs, and DVDs. Members of PM have founded enduring book fairs, spearheaded victorious tenant organizing campaigns, and worked closely with bookstores, academic conferences, and even rock bands to deliver political and challenging ideas to all walks of life. We're old enough to know what we're doing and young enough to know what's at stake.

We seek to create radical and stimulating fiction and nonfiction books, pamphlets, t-shirts, visual and audio materials to entertain, educate, and inspire you. We aim to distribute these through every available channel with every available technology, whether that means you are seeing anarchist classics at our bookfair stalls; reading our latest vegan cookbook at the café; downloading geeky fiction e-books; or digging new music and timely videos from our website.

PM Press is always on the lookout for talented and skilled volunteers, artists, activists and writers to work with. If you have a great idea for a project or can contribute in some way, please get in touch.

PM Press
PO Box 23912
Oakland, CA 94623
www.pmpress.org

Friends of PM

These are indisputably momentous times – the financial system is melting down globally and the Empire is stumbling. Now more than ever there is a vital need for radical ideas.

In the three years since its founding – and on a mere shoestring – PM Press has risen to the formidable challenge of publishing and distributing knowledge and entertainment for the struggles ahead. With over 150 releases to date, we have published an impressive and stimulating array of literature, art, music, politics, and culture. Using every available medium, we've succeeded in connecting those hungry for ideas and information to those putting them into practice.

Friends of PM allows you to directly help impact, amplify, and revitalize the discourse and actions of radical writers, filmmakers, and artists. It provides us with a stable foundation from which we can build upon our early successes and provides a much-needed subsidy for the materials that can't necessarily pay their own way. You can help make that happen - and receive every new title automatically delivered to your door once a month - by joining as a Friend of PM Press. And, we'll throw in a free T-Shirt when you sign up.

Here are your options:

▶ $25 a month: Get all books and pamphlets plus 50% discount on all webstore purchases

▶ $25 a month: Get all CDs and DVDs plus 50% discount on all webstore purchases

▶ $40 a month: Get all PM Press releases plus 50% discount on all webstore purchases

▶ $100 a month: **Superstar** – Everything plus PM merchandise, free downloads, and 50% discount on all webstore purchases

For those who can't afford $25 or more a month, we're introducing **Sustainer Rates** at $15, $10 and $5. Sustainers get a free PM Press t-shirt and a 50% discount on all purchases from our website.

Your Visa or Mastercard will be billed once a month, until you tell us to stop. Or until our efforts succeed in bringing the revolution around. Or the financial meltdown of Capital makes plastic redundant. Whichever comes first.

COOK, *EAT, THRIVE*

Vegan Recipes from Everyday to Exotic

JOY TIENZO

978-1-60486-509-7 • $17.95

In *Cook, Eat, Thrive*, Joy Tienzo encourages you to savor the cooking process while crafting distinctive meals from fresh, flavorful ingredients. Enjoy comfortable favorites. Broaden your culinary horizons with internationally inspired dishes. Share with friends and family, and create cuisine that allows people, animals, and the environment to fully thrive.

Drawing from a variety of influences, *Cook, Eat, Thrive* features a diversity of innovative vegan dishes, including well-known favorites like:

- Buttermilk Biscuits with Southern-Style Gravy
- Earl Grey–Carrot Muffins
- Palm Heart Ceviche
- Barbecue Ranch Salad
- Raspberry-Chèvre Salad with Champagne Vinaigrette
- Samosa Soup
- Mofongo with Cilantro Lime Gremolata
- Ras el Hanout–Roasted Beets
- Italian Cornmeal Cake with Roasted Apricots and Coriander Crème Anglaise
- Lavender Rice Pudding Brûlée with Blueberries

With planned menus for all occasions, clear symbols for recipes that are raw, low-fat, soy-free, and wheat-free, and a section on making basics like seitan and non-dairy milks, *Cook, Eat, Thrive* is an essential book for anyone interested in cooking the very best vegan food.

Joy Tienzo loves food, and writing about food. Whether working as a pastry cook, hosting community brunches, or crafting wedding cakes, her purpose in life is to feed as many people as well as possible. When not in the kitchen, Joy can be found on a plane, a yoga mat, or volunteering for refugee and human rights causes.

"*Cook, Eat, Thrive* gives vegans the option of choosing exotic and extraordinary recipes for special dinner preparations, or simpler, yet imaginative creations for day to day meal planning. Whether you're looking for everyday vegan fare, or exquisite vegan dining, Tienzo serves it up with culinary flair!"
—Dreena Burton, author of *Eat, Drink & Be Vegan*

NEW AMERICAN VEGAN

Vincent Guihan

978-1-60486-079-5 • $17.95

New American Vegan breaks from a steady stream of vegan cookbooks inspired by fusion and California cuisines that put catchy titles and esoteric ingredients first in their efforts to cater to a cosmopolitan taste. Instead, Vincent goes back to his Midwestern roots to play a humble but important role in the reinvention of American cuisine while bringing the table back to the center of American life.

Weaving together small-town values, personal stories, and more than 120 great recipes, *New American Vegan* delivers authentically American and authentically vegan cuisine that simply has to be tasted to be believed. Recipes range from very basic to the modestly complicated, but always focusing on creating something that is both beautiful and delicious while keeping it simple. Clear instructions provide step-by-steps but also help new cooks find their feet in a vegan kitchen, with a whole chapter devoted just to terms, tools, and techniques. With an eye toward improvisation, the book provides a detailed basic recipe that's good as-is, but also provides additional notes that explain how to take each recipe further, to increase flavor, to add drama to the presentation, or just how to add a little extra flourish for new cooks and seasoned kitchen veterans.

Vincent Guihan has been a vegan for more than a decade, and was a lacto-ovo vegetarian for a decade prior to becoming vegan. He grew up in a in a very small Midwestern town, where his back yard was the neighbor's cornfield. His parents cooked only sporadically, even though the nearest fast-food restaurants were a 20-minute car ride away and this cookbook is his revenge. He has been blogging about vegan cooking and gourmet topics since 2006. And although not a formally trained chef, he's a formally trained and highly skilled eater.

> "Guihan has a knack for infusing bold and fiery seasonings into fresh produce and vegan pantry staples--creating inventive, novel recipes that will inspire and excite the vegan home cook."
>
> —Dreena Burton, author of *Eat, Drink, & Be Vegan*

VEGAN FREAK

Being Vegan in a Non-Vegan World, 2nd Edition

Bob Torres and Jenna Torres

978-1-60486-015-3 • $14.95

Going vegan is easy, and even easier if you have the tools at hand to make it work right. In the second edition of this informative and practical guide, two seasoned vegans help you learn to love your inner vegan freak. Loaded with tips, advice, and stories, this book is the key to helping you thrive as a happy, healthy, and sane vegan in a decidedly non-vegan world that doesn't always get what you're about. In this sometimes funny, sometimes irreverent, and sometimes serious guide that's not afraid to tell it like it is, you will:

- find out how to go vegan in three weeks or less with our "cold tofu method"
- discover and understand the arguments for ethical, abolitionist veganism
- learn how to convince family and friends that you haven't joined a vegetable cult by going vegan
- get some advice on dealing with people in your life without creating havoc or hurt feelings
- learn to survive restaurants, grocery stores, and meals with omnivores
- find advice on how to respond when people ask if you "like, live on apples and twigs."

Now in a revised and expanded second edition, *Vegan Freak* is your guide to embracing vegan freakdom.

Bob Torres holds a PhD in Development Sociology from Cornell University. He's the author of *Making a Killing: The Political Economy of Animal Rights* and co-hosts Vegan Freak Radio.

Jenna Torres has a BA in Spanish and a BS in Plant Science from Penn State University, and received her PhD from Cornell University in Spanish linguistics. She is the co-host of Vegan Freak Radio, a podcast about life as a vegan in a very non-vegan world.

> "*Vegan Freak* is a witty, helpful, wall to wall look at going vegan. A must read for anyone who's felt like the only vegan freak in the room."
> —Sarah Kramer, author of *How It All Vegan*

GENERATION V

The Complete Guide to Going, Being, and Staying Vegan as a Teenager

Claire Askew

978-1-60486-338-3 • $14.95

Going vegan is not always easy when you are young. Living under your parents' roof, you probably do not buy your own groceries, and your friends, family, and teachers might look at you like you are nuts.

In this essential guide for the curious, aspiring, and current teenage vegan, Claire Askew draws on her years of experience as a teenage vegan and provides the tools for going vegan and staying vegan as a teen. Full of advice, stories, tips, and resources, Claire covers topics like: how to go vegan and stay sane; how to tell your parents so they do not freak out; how to deal with friends who do not get it; how to eat and stay healthy as a vegan; how to get out of dissection assignments in school; and tons more.

Whether you're a teenager who is thinking about going vegan or already vegan, this is the ultimate resource, written by someone like you, for you.

Claire Askew was born in 1990 and went vegan a few days after her 15th birthday. After growing up in the Midwest, she is currently studying English and gender at a small liberal arts college in Portland, OR.

"An essential guide that covers all bases... this first effort is a welcome surprise"
—VegNews

Cook Food

**a manualfesto for
easy, healthy, local eating**

Lisa Jervis

COOK FOOD

A Manualfesto for Easy, Healthy, Local Eating

Lisa Jervis

978-1-60486-073-3 • $12.00

More than just a rousing food manifesto and a nifty set of tools, *Cook Food* makes preparing tasty, wholesome meals simple and accessible for those hungry for both change and scrumptious fare. If you're used to getting your meals from a package—or the delivery guy—or if you think you don't know how to cook, this is the book for you.

If you want to eat healthier but aren't sure where to start, or if you've been reading about food politics but don't know how to bring sustainable eating practices into your everyday life, *Cook Food* will give you the scoop on how, while keeping your taste buds satisfied. With a conversational, do-it-yourself vibe, a practical approach to everyday cooking on a budget, and a whole bunch of animal-free recipes, *Cook Food* will have you cooking up a storm, tasting the difference, thinking globally and eating locally.

Lisa Jervis is the founding editor and publisher of *Bitch: Feminist Response to Pop Culture*, the founding board president of Women in Media and News, and a member of the advisory board for outLoud Radio. Her work has appeared in numerous magazines and books, including *Ms.*, *The San Francisco Chronicle*, *Utne*, *Mother Jones*, *Body Outlaws*, and *The Bust Guide to the New Girl Order*. She is the co-editor of *Young Wives' Tales: New Adventures in Love and Partnership*, and *Bitchfest: Ten Years of Cultural Criticism from the Pages of Bitch Magazine*. She's currently working on a book about the intellectual legacy of gender essentialism and its effect on contemporary feminism.

"*Cook Food* is what you would get if you combined CliffsNotes of Michael Pollan's foodie insta-classic *The Omnivore's Dilemma* with the vegan parts of Mark Bittman's *The Minimalist* cooking column in the *New York Times*, added a healthy pour of DIY attitude and ran it all through a blender. The book's subtitle calls it a 'manualfesto,' and that's just about right—it's a nitty-gritty how-to with a political agenda: to give those of us with good intentions but limited budgets, skills, confidence, or time a chance to participate in the burgeoning local food revolution."

—Salon.com

LICKIN' THE BEATERS 2

Vegan Chocolate and Candy

Siue Moffat • Illustrated by Celso and Missy Kulik

978-1-60486-009-2 • $17.95

The beaters go on—in *Lickin' the Beaters 2: Vegan Chocolate and Candy*, the second of Siue Moffat's fun vegan dessert cookbooks.

Themed around the duality of desert—an angel on one shoulder and a devil on the other—Siue takes chocolate, candy, and even ice creem (vegan alternative to ice cream) head-on with quirky illustrations, useful hints, and a handy "Quick Recipe" indicator to make using this book simple and amusing. With an understanding that dessert should be an indulgence, Moffat provides vegan renditions of tantalizing delicacies, both traditional and original.

Recipes include old favorites such as Caramel Corn, Salt Water Taffy, Pralines, Cookies, Cakes, and Fudge, as well as some brave new recipes like Fabulous Flourless Chocolate Torte and Toll-Free Chocolate Chip cookies.

Siue Moffat puts things on paper and film. She loves making vegan candy (she has started a chocolate truffle business) and inspecting beat-up film collections. Radical politics make her eyes light up and *Peanuts* comics make her giggle. Siue lives here and there and has a love/hate relationship with sugar and punk rock.

LICKIN' THE BEATERS

Low Fat Vegan Desserts

978-1-60486-004-7 • $10.95

Don't pass up dessert! If you're vegan or trying to eat healthy, there's no reason to deny yourself sweet treats. Lickin' the Beaters brings you over 80 fabulous low-fat, dairy-free desserts where even the second helping is guilt-free. Breads, cakes, donuts, candies, cookies and bars, pies, ice creams, puddings, toppings, fruity stuff, drinks, and a whole lot more. Illustrated with beautiful linocuts and zany cartoons, you'll find the recipes fun, easy to follow, and so good you'll eat half the batter.

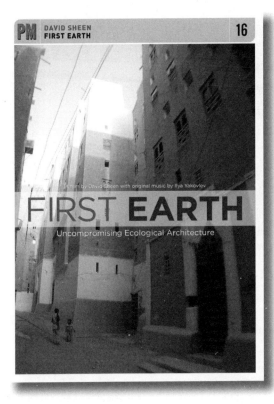

A film by David Sheen with original music by Ilya Yakovlev

FIRST **EARTH**

Uncompromising Ecological Architecture

FIRST EARTH

Uncompromising Ecological Architecture

David Sheen

978-1-60486-199-0 • $19.95 • DVD

A manifesto filmed over four years and four continents, this proposal contends that earthen homes—those made from cob, straw, clay, adobe bricks, and rammed earth—are the healthiest and best houses in the world. Also posing that suburban sprawl should be transformed into eco-villages, this discussion provides evidence of the benefits of this lifestyle in every cultural and socioeconomic context, from countrysides to urban jungles, third-world countries to tribal communities. Beautiful scenes of a myriad of cultures—curving art-poem dwellings in the Pacific Northwest, thousand-year-old Pueblo architecture in New Mexico, centuries-old and contemporary cob homes in England, thatched huts in West Africa, and Moorish-style skyscrapers in Yemen—make this global trek a testament to both the spiritual and material benefits of building with the earth.

This documentary film features appearances by renowned cultural observers and activists Derrick Jensen, Daniel Quinn, James Howard Kunstler, Richard Heinberg, Starhawk, and Mark Lakeman as well as major natural building teachers Michael G. Smith, Becky Bee, Joseph Kennedy, Sunray Kelly, and many more.

"This evocative and beautiful documentary shows why building with earth works well structurally, compels the eye and heart, is healthier for builders and dwellers than most other construction methods, and feels good to live in."
—Diana Leafe Christian, author of *Finding Community*

STUFFED AND STARVED

Raj Patel

978-1-60486-103-7 • $14.95 • CD

How can starving people also be obese?

Why does everything have soy in it?

How do petrochemicals and biofuels control the price of food?

It's a perverse fact of modern life: There are more starving people in the world than ever before (800 million) while there are also more people overweight (1 billion).

On this audio CD lecture, Patel talks about his comprehensive investigation into the global food network. It took him from the colossal supermarkets of California to India's wrecked paddy-fields and Africa's bankrupt coffee farms, while along the way he ate genetically-engineered soy beans and dodged flying objects in the protestor-packed streets of South Korea.

What he found was shocking, from the false choices given us by supermarkets to a global epidemic of farmer suicides, and real reasons for famine in Asia and Africa.

Yet he also found great cause for hope in international resistance movements working to create a more democratic, sustainable and joyful food system. Going beyond ethical consumerism, Patel explains, from seed to store to plate, the steps to regain control of the global food economy, stop the exploitation of both farmers and consumers, and rebalance global sustenance.

Raj Patel is a writer, activist and former policy analyst with Food First. He has worked for the World Bank, the WTO, and the United Nations, and has also protested them on four continents. He is the author of *Stuffed and Starved: The Hidden Battle for the World Food System.*

> "For anyone attempting to make sense of the world food crisis, or understand the links between U.S. farm policy and the ability of the world's poor to feed themselves, *Stuffed and Starved* is indispensable."
> —Michael Pollan, author of *The Omnivore's Dilemma* (on the book)

Also Available from PM Press

NONFICTION

500 Years of Indigenous Resistance	Gord Hill
The 5th Inning	E. Ethelbert Miller
About Face: Military Resisters Turn Against War	Buff and Cynthia Whitman-Bradley and Sarah Lazare
Against Architecture	Franco La Cecla
All Power to the Councils!: A Documentary History of the German Revolution of 1918–1919	Gabriel Kuhn, editor
Anarchism and Education: A Philosophical Perspective	Judith Suissa
Anarchist Pedagogies: Collective Actions, Theories, and Critical Reflections on Education	Robert H. Haworth, editor
Anarchist Seeds Beneath The Snow: Left-Libertarian Thought and British Writers from William Morris to Colin Ward	David Goodway
The Angry Brigade: A History of Britain's First Urban Guerilla Group	Gordon Carr
Arena One: On Anarchist Cinema	Richard Porton, editor
Arena Two: Anarchists in Fiction	Stuart Christie, editor
Asia's Unknown Uprisings Volume 1: South Korean Social Movements in the 20th Century	George Katsiaficas
Banksy Locations & Tours Volume 1: A Collection of Graffiti Locations and Photographs in London, England	Banksy and Bull Martin, editor
Banksy Locations & Tours Volume 2: A Collection of Graffiti Locations and Photographs from around the UK	Banksy and Bull Martin, editor
Black Flags and Windmills: Hope, Anarchy, and the Common Ground Collective	scott crow
Black Mask & Up Against the Wall Motherfucker: The Incomplete Works of Ron Hahne, Ben Morea, and the Black Mask Group	Ben Morea
Blood on the Tracks: The Life and Times of S. Brian Willson	S. Brian Willson
Burn Collector: Collected Stories from One through Nine	Al Burian
Capital and Its Discontents: Conversations with Radical Thinkers in a Time of Tumult	Sasha Lilley, editor
The CNT in the Spanish Revolution Volume 1	José Peirats
Creating a Movement with Teeth: A Documentary History of the George Jackson Brigade	Daniel Burton-Rose
Damned Fools in Utopia: And Other Writings on Anarchism and War Resistance	Nicolas Walter
Demanding the Impossible: A History of Anarchism	Peter Marshall
Diario de Oaxaca: A Sketchbook Journal of Two Years in Mexico	Peter Kuper
Don't Mourn, Balkanize!: Essays After Yugoslavia	Andrej Grubacic
Drawing the Line Once Again: Paul Goodman's Anarchist Writings	Paul Goodman
Enseñando Rebeldía: Historias de la Lucha Popular Oaxaqueña	Diana Denham and C.A.S.A Collective
Fire and Flames: A History of the German Autonomist Movement	Geronimo
The Floodgates of Anarchy	Stuart Christie and Albert Meltzer
For All the People: Uncovering the Hidden History of Cooperation, Cooperative Movements, and Communalism in America	John Curl
From Here to There: The Staughton Lynd Reader	Staughton Lynd
From the Bottom of the Heap: The Autobiography of Black Panther Robert Hillary King	Robert Hillary King
Global Slump: The Economics and Politics of Crisis and Resistance	David McNally
Gun Thugs, Rednecks, and Radicals: A Documentary History of the West Virginia Mine Wars	David Alan Corbin
How Shall I Live My Life?: On Liberating the Earth from Civilization	Derrick Jensen
In and Out of Crisis: The Global Financial Meltdown and Left Alternatives	Leo Panitch
Labor Law for the Rank and Filer 2nd Ed.: Building Solidarity While Staying Clear of the Law	Staughton Lynd and Daniel Gross
Labor's Civil War in California: The NUHW Healthcare Workers' Rebellion	Cal Winslow

What Would It Mean to Win?	Turbulence Collective
When Miners March	William C. Blizzard and edited by Wess Harris
William Morris: Romantic to Revolutionary	E.P. Thompson
Wobblies and Zapatistas: Conversations on Anarchism, Marxism, and Radical History	Staughton Lynd and Andrej Grubacic

FICTION/POETRY

Abe in Arms	Pegi Deitz Shea
Byzantium Endures: The First Volume of the Colonel Pyat Quartet	Michael Moorcock
Calling All Heroes: A Manual for Taking Power	Paco Ignacio Taibo II
The Chieu Hoi Saloon	Michael Harris
Dance the Eagle to Sleep: A Novel	Marge Piercy
Fire on the Mountain	Terry Bisson
Geek Mafia Series (including Black Hat Blues and Mile Zero)	Rick Dakan
Girls Are Not Chicks Coloring Book	Jacinta Bunnell, illustrated by Julie Novak
The Great Big Beautiful Tomorrow	Cory Doctorow
I-5: A Novel of Crime, Transport, and Sex	Summer Brenner
The Incredible Double	Owen Hill
Ivy, Homeless in San Francisco	Summer Brenner, illustrated by Brian Bowes
The Jook	Gary Phillips
The Left Left Behind	Terry Bisson
Lives Less Valuable	Derrick Jensen
Lonely Hearts Killer	Tomoyuki Hoshino
Low Bite	Sin Soracco
The Lucky Strike	Kim Stanley Robinson
Mammoths of the Great Plains	Eleanor Arnason
Mischief in the Forest: A Yarn Yarn	Derrick Jensen, illustrated by Stephanie McMillan
Modem Times 2.0	Michael Moorcock
A Moment of Doubt	Jim Nisbet
Operation Marriage	Cynthia Chin-Lee, illustrated by Lea Lyon
Pike	Benjamin Whitmer
The Primal Screamer	Nick Blinko
Prudence Couldn't Swim	James Kilgore
Send My Love and a Molotov Cocktail: Stories of Crime, Love and Rebellion	Gary Phillips and Andrea Gibbons
Sensation	Nick Mamatas
Sometimes the Spoon Runs Away with Another Spoon Coloring Book	Jacinta Bunnell, illustrated by Nathaniel Kusinitz
Songs of the Dead	Derrick Jensen
Surfing the Gnarl	Rudy Rucker
Suspended Somewhere Between: A Book of Verse	Akbar Ahmed
TVA Baby	Terry Bisson
The Underbelly	Gary Phillips
Vida	Marge Piercy
The Wild Girls	Ursula K. Le Guin
Wisdom Teeth	Derrick Weston Brown
The Wrong Thing	Barry Graham

PAMPHLETS

Abolish Restaurants: A Worker's Critique of the Food Service Industry	Prole.Info
Becoming The Media: A Critical History of Clamor Magazine	Jen Angel
COINTELSHOW: A Patriot Act	L.M. Bogad
Daring to Struggle, Failing to Win: The Red Army Faction's 1977 Campaign of Desperation	J. Smith and André Moncourt
The F-Word 03: A Feminist Handbook for the Revolution	Melody Berger
Organizing Cools the Planet: Tools and Reflections to Navigate the Climate Crisis	Joshua Kahn Russell and Hilary Moore
Prison Round Trip	Klaus Viehmann and Bill Dunne
The Prison-Industrial Complex and the Global Economy	Linda Evans and Eve Goldberg
Self-Defense for Radicals: A to Z Guide for Subversive Struggle	Mickey Z.
Sing for Your Supper: A DIY Guide to Playing Music, Writing Songs, and Booking Your Own Gigs	David Rovics
Solidarity Unionism at Starbucks	Staughton Lynd and Daniel Gross

AUDIO

1492–1992: The Legacy of Columbus	Howard Zinn
A Black & White Statement: The Story of the Rondos	Rondos
Blackwater: Mercenary Army	Jeremy Scahill
The Boy Bands Have Won	Chumbawamba
Crisis and Hope: Theirs and Ours (also available as DVD)	Noam Chomsky
English Rebel Songs 1381-1984	Chumbawamba
Get on With It: Live	Chumbawamba
Iraq: The Forever War	Noam Chomsky
The Liberty Tree: A Celebration of the Life and Writings of Thomas Paine	Leon Rosselson and Robb Johnson
The Mafia Principle of Global Hegemony: The Middle East, Empire & Activism (also available as DVD)	Noam Chomsky
Making Speech Free	Utah Phillips
The Meaning of Freedom	Angela Davis
Now This War Has Two Sides	Derrick Jensen
War and Civil Disobedience	Howard Zinn
The World Turned Upside Down: Rosselsongs 1960–2010	Leon Rosselson

VIDEO

The Angola 3: Black Panthers and the Last Slave Plantation	Jimmy O'Halligan, scott crow, and Ann Harkness
The Angry Brigade: The Spectacular Rise and Fall of Britain's First Urban Guerilla Group	Gordon Carr
Beyond Elections: Redefining Democracy in the Americas	Silvia Leindecker and Michael Fox
Black And Gold: The Story of the Almighty Latin King and Queen Nation	Big Noise Tactical Media
COINTELPRO 101	The Freedom Archives
Crossing the American Crises: From Collapse to Action	Silvia Leindecker and Michael Fox
END:CIV: Resist or Die	Franklin Lopez
The Fourth World War	Big Noise Tactical Media
Maria's Story: A Documentary Portrait of Love and Survival in El Salvador's Civil War	Pamela Cohen, Monona Wali, and Catherin Ryan
Positive Force: More Than a Witness: 25 Years of Punk Politics in Action	Robin Bell, Rachell Cain, and Brian Duss
The Rise of Disaster Capitalism	Naomi Klein
Theory and Practice: Conversations with Noam Chomsky and Howard Zinn	Sasha Lilley
This Is What Democracy Looks Like	Big Noise Tactical Media
Venezuela: Revolution from the Inside Out	Clifton Ross
Zapatista	Big Noise Tactical Media